Source Readings in Music History

Books by Oliver Strunk

Source Readings in Music History

Essays on Music in The Western World

Essays on Music in The Byzantine World

SOURCE READINGS IN MUSIC HISTORY

Antiquity and the Middle Ages

Selected and Annotated by
OLIVER STRUNK

W · W · NORTON & COMPANY

New York · London

Musical examples by Gordon Mapes

W. W. Norton & Company, Inc., 500 Fifth Avenue, New York, NY 10110
W. W. Norton & Company Ltd, 10 Coptic Street, London WC1A 1PU

ISBN 0-393-09680-7

PRINTED IN THE UNITED STATES OF AMERICA

2 3 4 5 6 7 8 9 0

To the Memory of
CARL ENGEL
1883–1944

ACKNOWLEDGMENTS

THE EDITOR wishes to acknowledge with thanks the co-operation of the following publishers who have granted permission to quote from works copyrighted by them: the Harvard University Press, for the selections from Plato, *The Republic*, Aristotle's *Politics*, Athenaeus, *The Deipnosophists*, Clement of Alexandria, and St. Augustine's *Confessions*, all from the Loeb Classical Library; and the Clarendon Press, Oxford, for a part of *The Harmonics of Aristoxenus* in the translation by Henry S. Macran. Acknowledgment is due also Donald C. Mackenzie, formerly of the Department of Classics at Princeton University, who was good enough to go over with the editor his translation from Cleonides.

ABBREVIATIONS

Grad. Vat.	*Graduale . . . de tempore et de sanctis* (Tournai, 1938)
Ant. Vat.	*Antiphonale . . . pro diurnis horis* (Rome, 1912)
	J. P. Migne, *Patrologia cursus completus.*
PL	—*Series latina.* 221 vols. (Paris, 1844–1855)
PG	—*Series graeca.* 166 vols. (Paris, 1857–1866)
GS	Martin Gerbert, *Scriptores ecclesiastici de musica.* 3 vols. (San Blasianis, 1784)
CS	C. E. H. Coussemaker, *Scriptorum de medii aevi nova series.* 4 vols. (Paris, 1864–1876)

Throughout the book, small letters refer to notes by the authors of the individual selections, arabic numerals to editor's notes. The abbreviation "*S.R.*" followed by a Roman numeral refers to another volume in the *Source Readings in Music History.*

Contents

I

THE GREEK VIEW OF MUSIC

II

THE EARLY CHRISTIAN VIEW OF MUSIC

III

MUSIC AS A LIBERAL ART

IV

MUSICAL THEORY IN THE MIDDLE AGES

Preface to the Five-Volume Edition

My *Source Readings in Music History*, a music-historical companion running to more than 900 pages and extending from classical antiquity through the romantic era, was originally published in 1950. That it is now being reissued in parts is due to a recognition, shared by the publishers and myself, that the usefulness of the book would be considerably enhanced if the readings for the single periods were also available separately and in a handier form. From the first, the aim had been to do justice to every age without giving to any a disproportionate share of the space. Thus the book has lent itself naturally to a division into parts, approximately equal in length, each part complete in itself. For use in the classroom, the advantages of the present edition are sufficiently obvious. For the casual reader, whose interest in the history of music is not likely to be all-inclusive, it will have other advantages, equally obvious. In the meantime, the original edition in one volume will remain in print and will be preferred by those who wish to have the whole between two covers, to be able to refer readily from one part of the book to another, and to be able to consult a single index.

In reprinting here the foreword to the edition of 1950, I have retained only those paragraphs that apply in some measure to all parts of the whole.

O. S.

Rome, 1965

Foreword

THIS BOOK began as an attempt to carry out a suggestion made in 1929 by Carl Engel in his *Views and Reviews*—to fulfil his wish for "a living record of musical personalities, events, conditions, tastes . . . a history of music faithfully and entirely carved from contemporary accounts." It owes something, too, to the well-known compilations of Kinsky and Schering and rather more, perhaps, to Andrea della Corte's *Antologia della storia della musica* and to an evaluation of this, its first model, by Alfred Einstein.

In its present form, however, it is neither the book that Engel asked for nor a literary anthology precisely comparable to the pictorial and musical ones of Kinsky and Schering, still less an English version of its Italian predecessor, with which it no longer has much in common. It departs from Engel's ideal scheme in that it has, at bottom, a practical purpose—to make conveniently accessible to the teacher or student of the history of music those things which he must eventually read. Historical documents being what they are, it inevitably lacks the seemingly unbroken continuity of Kinsky and Schering; at the same time, and for the same reason, it contains far more that is unique and irreplaceable than either of these. Unlike della Corte's book it restricts itself to historical documents as such, excluding the writing of present-day historians; aside from this, it naturally includes more translations, fewer original documents, and while recognizing that the somewhat limited scope of the *Antologia* was wholly appropriate in a book on music addressed to Italian readers, it seeks to take a broader view.

That, at certain moments in its development, music has been a subject of widespread and lively contemporary interest, calling forth a flood of documentation, while at other moments, perhaps not less critical, the records are either silent or unrevealing—this is in no way remarkable, for it is inherent in the very nature of music, of letters, and of history. The beginnings of the classical symphony and string quartet passed virtually unnoticed as developments without interest for the literary man; the beginnings of the opera and cantata, developments which concerned him immediately and deeply, were heralded and reviewed in documents so numerous that, even in a book of this size, it has been possible to include only the most significant. Thus, as already suggested, a documentary history of music cannot properly exhibit even the degree of continuity that is possible for an iconographic one or a collection of musical monuments, still less the degree expected of an interpretation. For this reason, too, I have rejected the simple chronological arrangement as inappropriate and misleading and have preferred to allow the documents to arrange themselves naturally under the various topics chronologically ordered in the Table of Contents and the book itself, some of these admirably precise, others perhaps rather too inclusive. As Engel shrewdly anticipated, the frieze has turned out to be incomplete, and I have left the gaps unfilled, as he wished.

For much the same reason, I have not sought to give the book a spurious unity by imposing upon it a particular point of view. At one time it is the musician himself who has the most revealing thing to say; at another time he lets someone else do the talking for him. And even when the musician speaks it is not always the composer who speaks most clearly; sometimes it is the theorist, at other times the performer. If this means that few readers will find the book uniformly interesting, it ought also to mean that "the changing patterns of life," as Engel called them, will be the more fully and the more faithfully reflected.

It was never my intention to compile a musical Bartlett, and I have accordingly sought, wherever possible, to include the complete text of the selection chosen, or—failing this—the complete text of a continuous, self-contained, and independently intelligible passage or series of passages, with or without regard for the chapter divisions of the original. But in a few cases I have made cuts to eliminate digressions or to avoid needless repetitions of things equally well said by earlier writers; in other cases the excessive length and involved construction of the original has forced me to abridge, reducing the scale of the whole while retaining the essential continuity of the argument. All cuts are clearly indicated, either by a row of dots or in annotations.

Without the lively encouragement and patient sympathy of the late William Warder Norton my work on this book would never have been begun. Nor is it at all likely that I would ever have finished it without the active collaboration of my father, William Strunk, Jr., Emeritus Professor of English at Cornell University, whose expert assistance and sound advice were constantly at my disposal during the earlier stages of its preparation and who continued to follow my work on it with the keenest interest until 1946, the year of his death. A considerable number of the translations now published for the first time are largely his work and there are few to which he did not make some improving contribution.

My warmest thanks are due to Professor Otto Kinkeldey, of Cornell University, and to Professor Alfred Einstein, of Smith College, for their extraordinary kindness in consenting to read the entire book in proof and for the many indispensable corrections and suggestions that they have sent me; again to Alfred Einstein, and to Paul Hindemith, for a number of constructive recommendations which grew out of their experiments with sections of the manuscript in connection with their teaching; likewise to my old friends Paul Lang, Arthur Mendel, and Erich Hertzmann, who have always been ready to listen and to advise.

Acknowledgment is due, also, to Dr. Dragan Plamenac, who prepared the greater number of the brief biographical notes which accompany the single readings; to two of my students—Philip Keppler, Jr., who relieved me of some part of the proofreading and J. W. Kerman, who prepared the index; to Gordon Mapes, for his careful work on the autographing of the musical examples; and to Miss Katherine Barnard, Miss Florence Williams, and the entire staff of W. W. Norton & Co., Inc., for their unflagging interest and innumerable kindnesses.

OLIVER STRUNK

The American Academy in Rome

I

The Greek View of Music

1. Plato

The great ancient Greek philosopher was born in 427 B.C. and died in 347 B.C. He must be considered the real founder of a philosophy of the arts in the modern sense of the word, although he derived his main ideas and method from the teachings of his eminent master Socrates.

After Socrates' death in 399 B.C., Plato started on extensive journeys, in the course of which he studied with Euclid. But he soon returned to Athens and began his career as a philosopher with writings in which he attacked the fallacious ideas on education propagated by the sophists. A crowd of students and enthusiastic followers gathered around him. About 390 Plato went to Sicily to become thoroughly acquainted with the Pythagorean doctrine and was well received at the court of Dionysius of Syracuse. After various unpleasant experiences, however, Plato returned to Athens, where he founded the so-called "Academy," a kind of school of higher studies, and spent his later life in restless scientific activity.

Plato's chief philosophical writings are not written in systematic form but take the shape of highly poetic and often dramatically vivid dialogues. The important figures of Greek public life in Plato's time make their appearance in them as representatives of their respective ideas. Socrates is regularly introduced as the moderator. One of the most famous dialogues from Plato's mature period is the one entitled *The Republic*. In this work the philosopher expounds his ideas about the organization of the ideal state. In such a state, as Plato conceives it, education is paramount and art derives its main value as a means of attaining this educational ideal. In this connection, Plato regards music as highly important; its lofty purpose is to serve, not for superficial entertainment, but to help in building up a harmonious personality and in calming the human passions.

From the Republic [1]

"AND NOW, my friend," said I, "we may say that we have completely finished the part of music that concerns speeches and tales. For we have set forth what is to be said and how it is to be said." "I think so too," he replied.

10. "After this, then," said I, "comes the manner of songs and melodies?" "Obviously." "And having gone thus far, could not everybody discover what we must say of their character in order to conform to what has already been said?" "I am afraid that 'everybody' does not include me," laughed Glaucon; "I cannot sufficiently divine offhand what we ought to say, though I have a suspicion." "You certainly, I presume," said I, "have a sufficient understanding of this—that the melody is composed of three things, the words, the harmony, and the rhythm?" [2] "Yes," said he, "that much." "And so far as it is words, it surely in no manner differs from words not sung in the requirement of conformity to the patterns and manner that we have prescribed?" "True," he said. "And again, the harmony and the rhythm must follow the words." "Of course." "But we said we did not require dirges and lamentations in words." "We do not." "What, then, are the dirge-like harmonies? Tell me, for you are a musician." [3]

1 Text: *The Republic*, I (London, W. Heinemann, 1930), 245–269, 287–295. Translated for the Loeb Classical Library by Paul Shorey. Reprinted by permission of Harvard University Press.

The speaker is the Platonic Socrates; in this discussion of the place of music in the education of the "guardians" he addresses himself to Glaucon, son of Ariston.

2 Cf. "And again, the harmony and the rhythm must follow the words"; "The rhythm and harmony follow the words and not the words these" (pp. 4 and 7 below). These remarks of Plato's are frequently cited in the sixteenth and seventeenth centuries as arguments against what Monteverdi calls "The First Practice"; see *S.R.* II, 66, 105; III, 18, 46 note d, and 54.

3 In the passage that follows, Plato enumerates six "harmonies," four of which he rejects on ethical grounds as unsuited for use in education. It should be read in the light of the comments of Aristotle in his *Politics* (1340B, 1341B–1342B, pp. 19, 23–24 below) and of Plutarch in his *De musica* (1136C–1137A).

The "harmonies" in question are precisely defined for us by Aristides Quintilianus, who writes them out in the vocal and instrumental notations

in the first book of his *De musica* (Meibom, pp. 21–22), where he has this to say of them:

"There are also other divisions of the tetrachord, and these the very oldest of the ancients used as harmonies. Sometimes they filled out the complete octochord; occasionally there was one that exceeded the scale of six tones; often there was one that fell short of it. For they did not always include all the notes; later on we shall give the reason why.

"To the Lydian scale they gave this form: diesis, ditone, tone, diesis, diesis, ditone, diesis; this was the complete scale.

"The Dorian had this form: tone, diesis, diesis, ditone, tone, diesis, diesis, ditone; this exceeded the diapason by a tone.

"The Phrygian had this form: tone, diesis, diesis, ditone, tone, diesis, diesis, tone; this was a complete diapason.

"To the Iastian they gave this form: diesis, diesis, ditone, trihemitone, tone; this fell short of the diapason by a tone.

"The Mixolydian had this form: two successive dieses, tone, tone, diesis, diesis, tritone; this was the complete scale.

"The so-called intense Lydian had this form: diesis, diesis, ditone, trihemitone.

"The Mixolydian," he said, "and the intense Lydian, and others similar to them." "These, then," said I, "we must do away with. For they are useless even to women who are to make the best of themselves, let alone to men." "Assuredly." "But again, drunkenness is a thing most unbefitting guardians, and so is softness and sloth." "Yes." "What, then, are the soft and convivial harmonies?" "There are certain Ionian and also Lydian ones that are called relaxed." "Will you make any use of them for warriors?" "None at all," he said; "but it would seem that you have left the Dorian and the Phrygian." "I don't know the harmonies," I said, "but leave us that [4] harmony that would fittingly imitate the utterances and the accents of a brave man who is engaged in warfare [5] or in any enforced business, and who, when he has failed, either meeting wounds or death or having fallen into some other mishap, in all these conditions confronts fortune with steadfast endurance and repels her strokes. And another for such a man engaged in works of peace, not enforced but voluntary, either trying to persuade somebody of something and imploring him—whether it be a god, through prayer, or a man, by teaching and admonition—or contrariwise yielding himself to another who is petitioning or teaching him or trying to change his opinions, and in consequence faring according to his wish, and not bearing himself arrogantly, but in all this acting modestly and moderately and acquiescing in the outcome. Leave us these two harmonies—the enforced and the voluntary—that will best imitate

"Thus the enharmonic diesis was to be heard in them all.

"To make things clear, a diagram of the scales is given below.

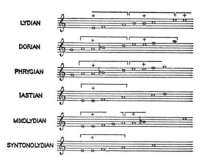

LYDIAN

DORIAN

PHRYGIAN

IASTIAN

MIXOLYDIAN

SYNTONOLYDIAN

"It is of these scales that the divine Plato speaks in his *Republic*, where he says that the Mixolydian and intense Lydian are dirge-like and the Iastian and Lydian convivial and too relaxed. Then he adds: 'You seem to be leaving out the Dorian and Phrygian.'

"For it was in this way that the ancients sought to explain their harmonies, matching the qualities of the sounds to the given material of the moral characters. On this point we shall speak more precisely later on."

For discussions of this testimony of Aristides, see J. F. Mountford's essays "Greek Music in Its Relation to Modern Times," in *Journal of Hellenic Studies*, XL (1920), 13–42 (especially 24–28), and "The Musical Scales of Plato's *Republic*," in *Classical Quarterly*, XVII (1923), 125–136; also R. P. Winnington-Ingram, *Mode in Ancient Greek Music* (Cambridge, 1936), pp. 21–30. Mountford, calling attention to Plutarch, *De musica*, 1136E, suggests that Aristides may have derived his information from the lost *De musica* of Aristoxenus; Winnington-Ingram connects the passage with the later remarks of Aristides (Meibom, pp. 95–96) on the nature of the harmonies "handed down" by Damon, Plato's authority in musical matters.

The testimony of Aristides is, of course, irreconcilable with the "pure-key view" of Greek music, and it is accordingly rejected as based upon forgery or misunderstanding by Monro, *The Modes of Ancient Greek Music* (Oxford, 1894), pp. 94–100, and Gombosi, *Tonarten und Stimmungen der antiken Musik* (Copenhagen, 1939), pp. 111–113.

[4] ἐκείνην (that) may mean, but does not say, Dorian. [Shorey]

[5] Monteverdi tells us (*S.R.* III, 53) that this characterization of the harmony suited to the brave man engaged in warfare prompted his discovery of the *stile concitato*.

the utterances of men failing or succeeding, the temperate, the brave— leave us these." "Well," said he, "you are asking me to leave none other than those I just spoke of." "Then," said I, "we shall not need in our songs and melodies an instrument of many strings or one on which all the harmonies can be played." "Not in my opinion," said he. "Then we shall not maintain makers of the trigonon, the pectis, or any other instrument which has many strings and can be played in many harmonies." "Apparently not." "Well, will you admit to the city makers and players of the aulos? Or is not the aulos the most 'many-stringed' of instruments and do not the pan-harmonics themselves imitate it?" "Clearly," he said. "You have left," said I, "the lyre and the cithara. These are useful in the city, and in the fields the shepherds would have a syrinx to pipe on." "So our argument indicates," he said. "We are not innovating, my friend, in preferring Apollo and the instruments of Apollo to Marsyas and his instruments." "No, by heaven!" he said, "I think not." "And by the dog," said I, "we have all unawares purged the city which a little while ago we said was wanton." "In that we show our good sense," he said.

11. "Come then, let us complete the purification. For upon harmonies would follow the consideration of rhythms: we must not pursue complexity nor great variety in the basic movements, but must observe what are the rhythms of a life that is orderly and brave, and after observing them require the foot and the melody to conform to that kind of man's speech and not the speech to the foot and the melody. What those rhythms would be, it is for you to tell us as you did the harmonies." "Nay, in faith," he said, "I cannot tell. For that there are some three forms from which the feet are combined, just as there are four in the notes of the voice whence come all harmonies, is a thing that I have observed and could tell. But which are imitations of which sort of life, I am unable to say." "Well," said I, "on this point we will take counsel with Damon, too,[6] as to which are the feet appropriate to illiberality, and insolence or madness or other evils, and what rhythms we must leave for their opposites; and I believe I have heard him obscurely speaking of a foot that he called the enoplios,[7] a composite foot, and a dactyl and an heroic foot, which he arranged, I know not how, to be equal up and down in the interchange of long and short,[8] and unless I am mistaken he used the term iambic, and there was another foot that he called the trochaic, and he added the quantities long

---

[6] Damon (see p. 4 above, note 3), the leading Athenian authority on music in Plato's time, is mentioned again in Book IV of the *Republic* (424C) as one who holds that musical styles cannot be disturbed without unsettling fundamental political and social conventions. There are further references to him in Plato's *Alcibiades I* (118C) and *Laches* (200B).

[7] Literally "in armor"—the rhythm of a warlike dance.

[8] Cf. the discussion of warlike and peaceful dancing in the *Laws*, 815E–816D.

and short. And in some of these, I believe, he censured and commended the tempo of the foot no less than the rhythm itself, or else some combination of the two; I can't say. But, as I said, let this matter be postponed for Damon's consideration. For to determine the truth of these would require no little discourse. Do you think otherwise?" "No, by heaven, I do not." "But this you are able to determine—that seemliness and unseemliness are attendant upon the good rhythm and the bad." "Of course." "And, further, that good rhythm and bad rhythm accompany, the one fair diction, assimilating itself thereto, and the other the opposite, and so of the apt and the unapt, if, as we were just now saying, the rhythm and harmony follow the words and not the words these." "They certainly must follow the words," he said. "And what of the manner of the diction, and the speech?" said I. "Do they not follow and conform to the disposition of the soul?" "Of course." "And all the rest to the diction?" "Yes." "Good speech, then, good accord, and good grace, and good rhythm wait upon a good disposition, not that weakness of head which we euphemistically style goodness of heart, but the truly good and fair disposition of the character and the mind." "By all means," he said. "And must not our youth pursue these everywhere if they are to do what it is truly theirs to do?" "They must indeed." "And there is surely much of these qualities in painting and in all similar craftsmanship—weaving is full of them and embroidery and architecture and likewise the manufacture of household furnishings and thereto the natural bodies of animals and plants as well. For in all these there is grace or gracelessness. And gracelessness and evil rhythm and disharmony are akin to evil speaking and the evil temper, but the opposites are the symbols and the kin of the opposites, the sober and good disposition." "Entirely so," he said.

12. "Is it, then, only the poets that we must supervise and compel to embody in their poems the semblance of the good character or else not write poetry among us, or must we keep watch over the other craftsmen, and forbid them to represent the evil disposition, the licentious, the illiberal, the graceless, either in the likeness of living creatures or in buildings or in any other product of their art, on penalty, if unable to obey, of being forbidden to practise their art among us, that our guardians may not be bred among symbols of evil, as it were in a pasturage of poisonous herbs, lest gazing freely and cropping from many such day by day they little by little and all unawares accumulate and build up a huge mass of evil in their own souls. But we must look for those craftsmen who by the happy gift of nature are capable of following the trail of true beauty and grace, that our young men, dwelling as it were in a salubrious region, may

receive benefit from all things about them, whence the influence that emanates from works of beauty may waft itself to eye or ear like a breeze that brings from wholesome places health, and so from earliest childhood insensibly guide them to likeness, to friendship, to harmony with beautiful reason." "Yes," he said, "that would be far the best education for them." "And is it not for this reason, Glaucon," said I, "that education in music is most sovereign, because more than anything else rhythm and harmony find their way to the inmost soul and take strongest hold upon it, bringing with them and imparting grace, if one is rightly trained, and otherwise the contrary? And further, because omissions and the failure of beauty in things badly made or grown would be most quickly perceived by one who was properly educated in music, and so, feeling distaste rightly, he would praise beautiful things and take delight in them and receive them into his soul to foster its growth and become himself beautiful and good. The ugly he would rightly disapprove of and hate while still young and yet unable to apprehend the reason, but when reason came the man thus nurtured would be the first to give her welcome, for by this affinity he would know her." "I certainly think," he said, "that such is the cause of education in music." "It is, then," said I, "as it was when we learned our letters and felt that we knew them sufficiently only when the separate letters did not elude us, appearing as few elements in all the combinations that convey them, and when we did not disregard them in small things or great and think it unnecessary to recognize them, but were eager to distinguish them everywhere, in the belief that we should never be literate and letter-perfect till we could do this." "True." "And is it not also true that if there are any likenesses of letters reflected in water or mirrors, we shall never know them until we know the originals, but such knowledge belongs to the same art and discipline?" "By all means." "Then, by heaven, am I not right in saying that by the same token we shall never be true musicians, either—neither we nor the guardians that we have undertaken to educate—until we are able to recognize the forms of soberness, courage, liberality, and high-mindedness and all their kindred and their opposites, too, in all the combinations that contain and convey them, and to apprehend them and their images wherever found, disregarding them neither in trifles nor in great things, but believing the knowledge of them to belong to the same art and discipline?" "The conclusion is inevitable," he said. "Then," said I, "when there is a coincidence of a beautiful disposition in the soul and corresponding and harmonious beauties of the same type in the bodily form—is not this the fairest spectacle for one who is capable of its contemplation?" "Far the fairest." "And surely the fairest is the most lovable." "Of course." "The true musician, then, would love by preference persons of this sort; but if there were disharmony he would not love this." "No," he said, "not if there was a defect in the soul; but if it were in the body he would bear with it and still be willing to bestow his love." "I understand," I said, "that you have or have had favorites of this sort and I grant your distinction. But tell me this—can there be any communion between soberness and extravagant pleasure?" "How could there be," he said, "since such pleasure puts a man beside himself no less than pain?" "Or between it and virtue generally?" "By no means." "But is there between pleasure and insolence and license?" "Most assuredly." "Do you know of greater or keener pleasure than that associated with Aphrodite?" "I don't," he said, "nor yet of any more insane." "But is not the right love a sober and harmonious love of the orderly and the beautiful?" "It is indeed," said he. "Then nothing of madness, nothing akin to license, must be allowed to come nigh the right love?" "No." "Then this kind of pleasure may not come nigh, nor may lover and beloved who rightly love and are loved have anything to do with it?" "No, by heaven, Socrates," he said, "it must not come nigh them." "Thus, then, as it seems, you will lay down the law in the city that we are founding, that the lover may kiss and pass the time with and touch the beloved as a father would a son, for honorable ends, if he persuade him. But otherwise he must so associate with the objects of his care that there should never be any suspicion of anything further, on penalty of being stigmatized for want of taste and true musical culture." "Even so," he said. "Do you not agree, then, that our discourse on music has come to an end? It has certainly made a fitting end, for surely the end and consummation of culture is the love of the beautiful." "I concur," he said.

13. "After music our youth are to be educated by gymnastics?" "Certainly." "In this too they must be carefully trained from boyhood through life, and the way of it is this, I believe; but consider it yourself too. For I, for my part, do not believe that a sound body by its excellence makes the soul good, but on the contrary that a good soul by its virtue renders the body the best that is possible. What is your opinion?" "I think so too." "Then if we should sufficiently train the mind and turn over to it the minutiae of the care of the body, and content ourselves with merely indicating the norms or patterns, not to make a long story of it, we should be acting rightly?" "By all means." "From intoxication we said that they

must abstain. For a guardian is surely the last person in the world to whom it is allowable to get drunk and not know where on earth he is." "Yes," he said, "it would be absurd that a guardian should need a guard." "What next about their food? These men are athletes in the greatest of contests, are they not?" "Yes." "Is, then, the bodily habit of the athletes we see about us suitable for such?" "Perhaps." "Nay," said I, "that is a drowsy habit and precarious for health. Don't you observe that they sleep away their lives, and that if they depart ever so little from their prescribed regimen these athletes are liable to great and violent diseases?" "I do." "Then," said I, "we need some more ingenious form of training for our athletes of war, since these must be as it were sleepless hounds, and have the keenest possible perceptions of sight and hearing, and in their campaigns undergo many changes in their drinking water, their food, and in exposure to the heat of the sun and to storms, without disturbance of their health." "I think so." "Would not, then, the best gymnastics be akin to the music that we were just now describing?" "What do you mean?" "It would be a simple and flexible gymnastic, and especially so in the training for war." "In what way?" "One could learn that," said I, "even from Homer. For you are aware that in the banqueting of the heroes on campaign he does not feast them on fish, though they are at the sea-side on the Hellespont, nor on boiled meat, but only on roast, which is what soldiers could most easily procure. For everywhere, one may say, it is of easier provision to use the bare fire than to convey pots and pans along." "Indeed it is." "Neither, as I believe, does Homer ever make mention of sweetmeats. Is not that something which all men in training understand—that if one is to keep his body in good condition he must abstain from such things altogether?" "They are right," he said, "in that they know it and do abstain." "Then, my friend, if you think this is the right way, you apparently do not approve of a Syracusan table and Sicilian variety of made dishes." "I think not." "You would frown, then, on a little Corinthian maid as the *chère amie* of men who were to keep themselves fit?" "Most certainly." "And also on the seeming delights of Attic pastry?" "Inevitably." "In general, I take it, if we likened that kind of food and regimen to music and song expressed in the 'pan-harmonic' and in every variety of rhythm it would be a fair comparison." "Quite so." "And there variety engendered licentiousness, did it not, but here disease? While simplicity in music begets sobriety in the souls, and in gymnastic training it begets health in bodies." "Most true," he said. "And when licentiousness and disease multiply in a city, are not many courts of law and dispensaries opened, and the arts of chicane and medicine give themselves airs when even free men in great numbers take them very seriously?" "How can they help it?" he said.

. . . . .

"And so your youths," said I, "employing that simple music which we said engendered sobriety will, it is clear, guard themselves against falling into the need of the justice of the courtroom." "Yes," he said. "And will not our musician, pursuing the same trail in his use of gymnastics, if he please, get to have no need of medicine save when indispensable?" "I think so." "And even the exercises and toils of gymnastics he will undertake with a view to the spirited part of his nature to arouse that rather than for mere strength, unlike ordinary athletes, who treat diet and exercise only as a means to muscle." "Nothing could be truer," he said. "Then may we not say, Glaucon," said I, "that those who established an education in music and gymnastics had not the purpose in view that some attribute to them in so instituting, namely to treat the body by one and the soul by the other?" "But what?" he said. "It seems likely," I said, "that they ordained both chiefly for the soul's sake." "How so?" "Have you not observed," said I, "the effect on the disposition of the mind itself of lifelong devotion to gymnastics with total neglect of music? Or the disposition of those of the opposite habit?" "In what respect do you mean?" he said. "In respect of savagery and hardness or, on the other hand, of softness and gentleness?" "I have observed," he said, "that the devotees of unmitigated gymnastics turn out more brutal than they should be and those of music softer than is good for them." "And surely," said I, "this savagery is a quality derived from the high-spirited element in our nature, which, if rightly trained, becomes brave, but if overstrained, would naturally become hard and harsh." "I think so," he said. "And again, is not the gentleness a quality which the philosophic nature would yield? This if relaxed too far would be softer than is desirable but if rightly trained gentle and orderly?" "That is so." "But our requirement, we say, is that the guardians should possess both natures." "It is." "And must they not be harmoniously adjusted to one another?" "Of course." "And the soul of the man thus attuned is sober and brave?" "Certainly." "And that of the ill adjusted is cowardly and rude?" "It surely is."

18. "Now when a man abandons himself to music to play upon him and pour into his soul as it were through the funnel of his ears those sweet, soft, and dirge-like harmonies of which we were just now speaking, and gives his entire time to the warblings and blandishments of song, the first result is that the principle of high spirit, if he had it, is softened like

iron and is made useful instead of useless and brittle. But when he continues the practice without remission and is spellbound, the effect begins to be that he melts and liquefies till he completely dissolves away his spirit, cuts out as it were the very sinews of his soul and makes of himself a 'feeble warrior.'" "Assuredly," he said. "And if," said I, "he has to begin with a spiritless nature he reaches this result quickly, but if a high-spirited, by weakening the spirit he makes it unstable, quickly irritated by slight stimuli, and as quickly quelled. The outcome is that such men are choleric and irascible instead of high-spirited, and are peevish and discontented." "Precisely so." "On the other hand, if a man toils hard at gymnastics and eats right lustily and holds no truck with music and philosophy, does he not at first get very fit and full of pride and high spirit and become more brave and bold than he was?" "He does indeed." "But what if he does nothing but this and has no contact with the Muse in any way, is not the result that even if there was some principle of the love of knowledge in his soul, since it tastes of no instruction nor of any inquiry and does not participate in any discussion or any other form of culture, it becomes feeble, deaf, and blind, because it is not aroused or fed nor are its perceptions purified and quickened?" "That is so," he said. "And so such a man, I take it, becomes a misologist and a stranger to the Muses. He no longer makes any use of persuasion by speech but achieves all his ends like a beast by violence and savagery, and in his brute ignorance and ineptitude lives a life of disharmony and gracelessness." "That is entirely true," he said. "For these two, then, it seems there are two arts which I would say some god gave to mankind, music and gymnastics for the service of the high-spirited principle and the love of knowledge in them—not for the soul and the body except incidentally, but for the harmonious adjustment of these two principles by the proper degree of tension and relaxation of each." "Yes, so it appears," he said. "Then he who best blends gymnastics with music and applies them most suitably to the soul is the man whom we should most rightly pronounce to be the most perfect and harmonious musician, far rather than the one who brings the strings into unison with one another." "That seems likely, Socrates," he said. "And shall we not also need in our city, Glaucon, a permanent overseer of this kind if its constitution is to be preserved?" "We most certainly shall."

2. Aristotle

One of the most influential and versatile of thinkers, Aristotle was a "philosopher, psychologist, logician, moralist, political thinker, biologist, the founder of literary criticism." He was born in 384 B.C. in Stagira, a Greek colonial town on the Aegean Sea, and became a pupil and later a teacher at Plato's Academy in Athens. In 343 he was invited by Philip of Macedonia to supervise the education of Philip's son Alexander. After Alexander's ascension to the throne Aristotle returned to Athens and founded there the so-called "Peripatetic School" in the Lyceum. After Alexander's death Aristotle was obliged to leave Athens for political reasons and died in 322 B.C. on his country estate near Chalcis on the island of Euboea.

Aristotle's preserved works were probably written during the last twelve years of his life. They encompass nearly the entire range of the knowledge of his day. The *Politics* is a fragment of an extensive work on the *Constitutions*.

The influence of Aristotelian doctrine in the history of philosophy of the Western world has been immense. In the Middle Ages, Aristotle became the supreme philosophical authority. Yet his ideas remained imperfectly understood until the beginnings of textual criticism in the Renaissance.

From the Politics [1]

2. IT IS therefore not difficult to see that the young must be taught those useful arts that are indispensably necessary; but it is clear that they should not be taught all the useful arts, those pursuits that are liberal being kept distinct from those that are illiberal, and that they must participate in such among the useful arts as will not render the person who participates in them vulgar. A task and also an art or a science must be deemed vulgar if it renders the body or soul or mind of free men useless for the employ-

1 Text: *The Politics* (London, W. Heinemann, 1932), pp. 637–645, 649–675. Translated for the Loeb Classical Library by H. Rackham. Reprinted by permission of Harvard University Press.

ments and actions of virtue. Hence we entitle vulgar all such arts as deteriorate the condition of the body, and also the industries that earn wages; for they make the mind preoccupied and degraded. And even with the liberal sciences, although it is not illiberal to take part in some of them up to a point, to devote oneself to them too assiduously and carefully is liable to have the injurious results specified. Also it makes much difference what object one has in view in a pursuit or study; if one follows it for the sake of oneself or one's friends, or on moral grounds, it is not illiberal, but the man who follows the same pursuit because of other people would often appear to be acting in a menial and servile manner.

The branches of study at present established fall into both classes, as was said before. There are perhaps four customary subjects of education, reading and writing, gymnastics, music, and fourth, with some people, drawing; reading and writing and drawing being taught as being useful for the purposes of life and very serviceable, and gymnastics as contributing to manly courage; but as to music here one might raise a question. For at present most people take part in it for the sake of pleasure; but those who originally included it in education did so because, as has often been said, nature itself seeks to be able not only to engage rightly in business but also to occupy leisure nobly; for—to speak about it yet again— this is the first principle of all things. For if although both business and leisure are necessary, yet leisure is more desirable and more fully an end than business, we must inquire what is the proper occupation of leisure. For assuredly it should not be employed in play,[2] since it would follow that play is our end in life. But if this is impossible, and sports should rather be employed in our times of business (for a man who is at work needs rest, and rest is the object of play, while business is accompanied by toil and exertion), it follows that in introducing sports we must watch the right opportunity for their employment, since we are applying them to serve as medicine; for the activity of play is a relaxation of the soul, and serves as recreation because of its pleasantness. But leisure seems itself to contain pleasure and happiness and felicity of life. And this is not possessed by the busy but by the leisured; for the busy man busies himself for the sake of some end as not being in his possession, but happiness is an end achieved, which all men think is accompanied by pleasure and not by pain. But all men do not go on to define this pleasure in the same way, but ac-

---

2 The distinction between "play," "sport," or "amusement" (παιδιά) and "pastime" or "entertainment" (διαγωγή) is essential to Aristotle's argument. "Amusement" is recreation, a restful and relaxing activity in spare time; "entertain- ment" is the employment of leisure. "Amusement" belongs to the worker, "entertainment" to the free man; "amusement" is useful, "entertainment" liberal.

cording to their various natures and to their own characters, and the pleasure with which the best man thinks that happiness is conjoined is the best pleasure and the one arising from the noblest sources. So that it is clear that some subjects must be learnt and acquired merely with a view to the pleasure in their pursuit, and that these studies and these branches of learning are ends in themselves, while the forms of learning related to business are studied as necessary and as means to other things. Hence our predecessors included music in education not as a necessity (for there is nothing necessary about it), nor as useful (in the way in which reading and writing are useful for business and for household management and for acquiring learning and for many pursuits of civil life, while drawing also seems to be useful in making us better judges of the works of artists), nor yet again as we pursue gymnastics for the sake of health and strength (for we do not see either of these things produced as a result of music); it remains therefore that it is useful as a pastime in leisure, which is evidently the purpose for which people actually introduce it, for they rank it as a form of pastime that they think proper for free men. For this reason Homer wrote thus:

> But him alone
> 'Tis meet to summon to the festal banquet; [3]

and after these words he speaks of certain others

> Who call the bard that he may gladden all. [4]

And also in other verses Odysseus says that this is the best pastime, when, as men are enjoying good cheer,

> The banqueters, seated in order due
> Throughout the hall may hear a minstrel sing. [5]

3. It is clear therefore that there is a form of education in which boys should be trained not because it is useful or necessary but as being liberal and noble; though whether there is one such subject of education or several, and what these are and how they are to be pursued, must be discussed later, but as it is we have made this much progress on the way, that we have some testimony even from the ancients, derived from the courses of education which they founded—for the point is proved by music. And it is also clear that some of the useful subjects as well ought to be studied by the young not only because of their utility, like the study of reading and writing, but also because they may lead on to many other

[3] Corresponds to *Odyssey*, XVII, 385, but not exactly. [Rackham]

[4] This line is not in our *Odyssey*, but apparently followed XVII, 383. [Rackham]
[5] *Odyssey*, IX, 5–6.

branches of knowledge; and similarly they should study drawing not in order that they may not go wrong in their private purchases and may avoid being cheated in buying and selling furniture, but rather because this study makes a man observant of bodily beauty; and to seek for utility everywhere is entirely unsuited to men that are great-souled and free. And since it is plain that education by habit must come before education by reason, and training of the body before training of the mind, it is clear from these considerations that the boys must be handed over to the care of the wrestling-master and the trainer; for the latter imparts a certain quality to the habit of the body and the former to its actions.

·   ·   ·   ·   ·

About music on the other hand we have previously raised some questions in the course of our argument, but it is well to take them up again and carry them further now, in order that this may give the key so to speak for the principles which one might advance in pronouncing about it. For it is not easy to say precisely what potency it possesses, nor yet for the sake of what object one should participate in it—whether for amusement and relaxation, as one indulges in sleep and deep drinking (for these in themselves are not serious pursuits but merely pleasant, and "relax our cares," as Euripides says [6]; owing to which people actually class music with them and employ all of these things, sleep, deep drinking, and music, in the same way, and they also place dancing in the same class); or whether we ought rather to think that music tends in some degree to virtue (music being capable of producing a certain quality of character just as gymnastics are capable of producing a certain quality of body, music accustoming men to be able to rejoice rightly); or that it contributes something to intellectual entertainment and culture (for this must be set down as a third alternative among those mentioned). Now it is not difficult to see that one must not make amusement the object of the education of the young; for amusement does not go with learning—learning is a painful process. Nor yet moreover is it suitable to assign intellectual entertainment to boys and to the young; for a thing that is an end does not belong to anything that is imperfect. But perhaps it might be thought that the serious pursuits of boys are for the sake of amusement when they have grown up to be men. But if something of this sort is the case, why should the young need to learn this accomplishment themselves, and not, like the Persian and Median kings, participate in the pleasure and the education of music by means of others performing it? for those who have made music a business and profession must necessarily perform better than those who practise only long enough to learn. But if it is proper for them to labor at accomplishments of this sort, then it would also be right for them to prepare the dishes of an elaborate cuisine; but this is absurd. And the same difficulty also arises as to the question whether learning music can improve their characters; for why should they learn to perform edifying music themselves, instead of learning to enjoy it rightly and be able to judge it when they hear others performing, as the Spartans do? for the Spartans although they do not learn to perform can nevertheless judge good and bad music correctly, so it is said. And the same argument applies also if music is to be employed for refined enjoyment and entertainment; why need people learn to perform themselves instead of enjoying music played by others? And we may consider the conception that we have about the gods: Zeus does not sing and harp to the poets himself. But professional musicians we speak of as vulgar people, and indeed we think it not manly to perform music, except when drunk or for fun.

5. But perhaps these points will have to be considered afterwards; our first inquiry is whether music ought not or ought to be included in education, and what is its efficacy among the three uses of it that have been discussed—does it serve for education or amusement or entertainment? It is reasonable to reckon it under all of these heads, and it appears to participate in them all. Amusement is for the sake of relaxation, and relaxation must necessarily be pleasant, for it is a way of curing the pain due to laborious work; also entertainment ought admittedly to be not only honorable but also pleasant, for happiness is derived from both honor and pleasure; but we all pronounce music to be one of the pleasantest things, whether instrumental or instrumental and vocal music together (at least Musaeus says, "Song is man's sweetest joy," [7] and that is why people with good reason introduce it at parties and entertainments, for its exhilarating effect), so that for this reason also one might suppose that the younger men ought to be educated in music. For all harmless pleasures are not only suitable for the ultimate object but also for relaxation; and as it but rarely happens for men to reach their ultimate object, whereas they often relax and pursue amusement not so much with some ulterior object but because of the pleasure of it, it would be serviceable to let them relax at intervals in the pleasures derived from music. But it has come about that men make amusements an end; for the end also perhaps contains a certain pleasure, but not any ordinary pleasure, and seeking this they take the other as being this because it has a certain resemblance to the achievement of the end of their undertakings. For the end is desirable not for the sake of anything

7 A semi-legendary bard, to whom a number of oracular verses that were current were attributed. [Rackham]

that will result from it, and also pleasures of the sort under consideration are not desirable for the sake of some future result, but because of things that have happened already, for instance labor and pain. One might then perhaps assume this to be the reason which causes men to seek to procure happiness by means of those pleasures; but in the case of taking part in music, this is not because of this reason only, but also because performing music is useful, as it seems, for relaxation. But nevertheless we must examine whether it is not the case that, although this has come about, yet the nature of music is more honorable than corresponds with the employment of it mentioned, and it is proper not only to participate in the common pleasure that springs from it, which is perceptible to everybody (for the pleasure contained in music is of a natural kind, owing to which the use of it is dear to those of all ages and characters), but to see if its influence reaches also in a manner to the character and to the soul. And this would clearly be the case if we are affected in our characters in a certain manner by it. But it is clear that we are affected in a certain manner, both by many other kinds of music and not least by the melodies of Olympus; [8] for these admittedly make our souls enthusiastic, and enthusiasm is an affection of the character of the soul. And moreover everybody when listening to imitations is thrown into a corresponding state of feeling, even apart from the rhythms and melodies themselves.[9] And since it is the case that music is one of the things that give pleasure, and that virtue has to do with feeling delight and love and hatred rightly, there is obviously nothing that is more needful to learn and become habituated to than to judge correctly and to delight in virtuous characters and noble actions; but rhythms and melodies contain representations of anger and mildness, and also of courage and temperance and all their opposites and the other moral qualities, that most closely correspond to the true natures of these qualities (and this is clear from the facts of what occurs—when we listen to such representations we change in our soul); and habituation in feeling pain and delight at representations of reality is close to feeling them towards actual reality (for example, if a man delights in beholding the statue of somebody for no other reason than because of its actual form, the actual sight of the person whose statue he beholds must also of necessity give him pleasure); and it is the case that whereas the other objects of sensation contain no representation of character, for example the objects of touch and taste (though

8 Phrygian melodies; see p. 19 below, where the Phrygian harmony is said to have the power of arousing enthusiasm.

9 A probable correction of the Greek gives "by the rhythms and melodies themselves, even apart from the words." [Rackham].

Unlike Plato, Aristotle considers purely instrumental music a legitimate "mode of imitation" (cf. *Poetics*, i, 4–5; *Problems*, 919B [Problem 27]).

the objects of sight do so slightly, for there are forms that represent character, but only to a small extent, and not all men participate in visual perception of such qualities; also visual works of art are not representations of character but rather the forms and colors produced are mere indications of character, and these indications are only bodily sensations during the emotions; not but what in so far as there is a difference even in regard to the observation of these indications, the young must not look at the works of Pauson, but those of Polygnotus [10] and of any other moral painter or sculptor), pieces of music on the contrary do actually contain in themselves imitations of character; and this is manifest, for even in the nature of the mere harmonies there are differences, so that people when hearing them are affected differently and have not the same feelings in regard to each of them, but listen to some in a more mournful and restrained state, for instance the harmony called Mixolydian, and to others in a softer state of mind, for instance the relaxed harmonies, but in a midway state and with the greatest composure to another, as the Dorian alone of harmonies seems to act, while the Phrygian makes men enthusiastic; [11] for these things are well stated by those who have studied this form of education, as they derive the evidence for their theories from the actual facts of experience. And the same holds good about the rhythms also, for some have a more stable and others a more emotional character, and of the latter some are more vulgar in their emotional effects and others more liberal. From these considerations therefore it is plain that music has the power of producing a certain effect on the moral character of the soul, and if it has the power to do this, it is clear that the young must be directed to music and must be educated in it. Also education in music is well adapted to the youthful nature; for the young owing to their youth cannot endure anything not sweetened by pleasure, and music is by nature a thing that has a pleasant sweetness. And we seem to have a certain affinity with harmonies and rhythms; owing to which many wise men say either that the soul is a harmony or that it has harmony.[12]

6. We ought now to decide the question raised earlier, whether the young ought to learn music by singing and playing themselves or not. It is not difficult to see that it makes a great difference in the process of acquiring a certain quality whether one takes a part in the actions that impart it oneself; for it is a thing that is impossible, or difficult, to become a

---

10 "Polygnotus represented men as better than they really were, Pauson as worse." (*Poetics*, 1448A)

11 This fourfold classification of the "harmonies" according to their ethical character repeats the classification of Plato (*Republic*, 398D–399A, pp. 4–6 above).

12 Cf. Plato, *Republic*, 401D (pp. 8–9 above); also *Republic*, 443D–443E; *Timaeus*, 47D–47E; *Phaedo*, 85–95; for Aristotle's criticism see his *De anima*, 407B–408A.

good judge of performances if one has not taken part in them. At the same time also boys must have some occupation, and one must think Archytas's rattle [13] a good invention, which people give to children in order that while occupied with this they may not break any of the furniture; for young things cannot keep still. Whereas then a rattle is a suitable occupation for infant children, education serves as a rattle for young people when older. Such considerations therefore prove that children should be trained in music so as actually to take part in its performance; and it is not difficult to distinguish what is suitable and unsuitable for various ages, and to refute those who assert that the practice of music is vulgar. For first, inasmuch as it is necessary to take part in the performances for the sake of judging them, it is therefore proper for the pupils when young actually to engage in the performances, though when they get older they should be released from performing, but be able to judge what is beautiful and enjoy it rightly because of the study in which they engaged in their youth. Then as to the objection raised by some people that music makes people vulgar, it is not difficult to solve it by considering how far pupils who are being educated with a view to civic virtue should take part in the actual performance of music, and in what melodies and what rhythms they should take part, and also what kinds of instruments should be used in their studies, as this naturally makes a difference. For the solution of the objection depends upon these points, as it is quite possible that some styles of music do produce the result mentioned. It is manifest therefore that the study of music must not place a hindrance in the way of subsequent activities, nor vulgarize the bodily frame and make it useless for the exercises of the soldier and the citizen, either for their practical pursuit now or for their scientific study later on. And this would come about in respect of their study if the pupils did not go on toiling at the exercises that aim at professional competitions, nor the wonderful and elaborate performances which have now entered into the competitions and have passed from the competitions into education, but also only practised exercises not of that sort until they are able to enjoy beautiful melodies and rhythms, and not merely the charm common to all music, which even some lower animals enjoy, as well as a multitude of slaves and children. And it is also clear from these considerations what sort of instruments they should use. The auloi must not be introduced into education, nor any other profes-

---

13 A Pythagorean philosopher, mathematician, statesman, and general of Tarentum, contemporary with Plato. He was interested in mechanics; but one tradition ascribes the toy in question to a carpenter of the same name. [Rackham]
To Archytas are also due the earliest divisions of the tetrachord that have come down to us, and Reinach plausibly attributes to him or to his circle the fixation, if not the actual invention of the Greek musical notation (cf. his *Musique grecque*, Paris, 1926, pp. 26 and 163).

sional instrument, such as the cithara or any other of that sort, but such instruments as will make them attentive pupils either at their musical training or in their other lessons. Moreover the aulos is not a moralizing but rather an exciting influence, so that it ought to be used for occasions of the kind at which attendance has the effect of purification rather than instruction. And let us add that the aulos happens to possess the additional property telling against its use in education that playing it prevents the employment of speech. Hence former ages rightly rejected its use by the young and the free, although at first they had employed it. For as they came to have more leisure because of their wealth and grew more high-spirited and valorous, both at a still earlier date and because after the Persian wars they were filled with pride as a result of their achievements, they began to engage in all branches of learning, making no distinction but pursuing research further. Because of this they even included aulos-playing among their studies; for in Sparta a certain chorus-leader played the aulos to his chorus himself, and at Athens it became so fashionable that almost the majority of freemen went in for aulos-playing, as is shown by the tablet erected by Thrasippus after having provided the chorus for Ecphantides. But later on it came to be disapproved of as a result of actual experience, when men were more capable of judging what music conduced to virtue and what did not; and similarly also many of the old instruments were disapproved of, like the pectis and the barbitos and the instruments designed to give pleasure to those who hear people playing them, the heptagonon, the trigonon, and the sambyca, and all the instruments that require manual skill. And indeed there is a reasonable foundation for the story that was told by the ancients about the auloi. The tale goes that Athene found a pair of auloi and threw them away. Now it is not a bad point in the story that the goddess did this out of annoyance because of the ugly distortion of her features; but as a matter of fact it is more likely that it was because education in aulos-playing has no effect on the intelligence, whereas we attribute science and art to Athene.

7. And since we reject professional education in the instruments and in performance [14] (and we count performance in competitions as professional, for the performer does not take part in it for his own improvement, but for his hearers' pleasure, and that a vulgar pleasure, owing to which we do not consider performing to be proper for free men, but somewhat menial; and indeed performers do become vulgar, since the object at which they aim is a low one, as vulgarity in the audience usually in-

---

[14] The Greek should probably be altered to read "reject some instruments and professional education in performance." [Rackham]

fluences the music, so that it imparts to the artists who practise it with a
view to suit the audience a special kind of personality, and also of bodily
frame because of the movements required)—we must therefore give some
consideration to harmonies and rhythms, and to the question whether for
educational purposes we must employ all the harmonies and all the
rhythms or make distinctions; and next, whether for those who are
working at music for education we shall lay down the same regulation,
or ought we to establish some other third one (inasmuch as we see that
the factors in music are melody and rhythm, and it is important to notice
what influence each of these has upon education), and whether we are
to prefer music with a good melody or music with a good rhythm. Now we
consider that much is well said on these matters by some of the musicians
of the present day and by some of those engaged in philosophy who happen to be experienced in musical education, and we will abandon the precise discussion as to each of these matters for any who wish it to seek it from
those teachers, while for the present let us lay down general principles,
merely stating the outlines of the subjects. And since we accept the classification of melodies made by some philosophers, as ethical melodies, melodies of action, and passionate melodies, distributing the various harmonies
among these classes as being in nature akin to one or the other,[15] and as
we say that music ought to be employed not for the purpose of one benefit
that it confers but on account of several (for it serves the purpose both of
education and of purgation—the term purgation we use for the present
without explanation, but we will return to discuss the meaning that we
give to it more explicitly in our treatise on poetry—and thirdly it serves
for amusement, serving to relax our tension and to give rest from it), it
is clear that we should employ all the harmonies, yet not employ them all
in the same way, but use the most ethical ones for education, and the active
and passionate kinds for listening to when others are performing (for any
experience that occurs violently in some souls is found in all, though with
different degrees of intensity—for example pity and fear, and also religious excitement; for some persons are very liable to this form of emo-
tion, and under the influence of sacred music we see these people, when
they use melodies that violently arouse the soul, being thrown into a state
as if they had received medicinal treatment and taken a purge; the same
experience then must come also to the compassionate and the timid and
the other emotional people generally in such degree as befalls each individual of these classes, and all must undergo a purgation and a pleasant

15 Literally "ethical, practical, and enthusiastic." Beyond characterizing the Dorian as "ethical" (p. 15 below) and the Phrygian as "enthusiastic" (pp. 18–19 above), Aristotle does not tell
us how the harmonies are to be distributed among
these classes.

feeling of relief; and similarly also the purgative melodies afford harmless delight to people). Therefore those who go in for theatrical music must be set to compete in harmonies and melodies of this kind (and since the audience is of two classes, one freemen and educated people, and the other the vulgar class composed of mechanics and laborers and other such persons, the latter sort also must be assigned competitions and shows for relaxation; and just as their souls are warped from the natural state, so those harmonies and melodies that are intense and irregular in coloration are deviations, but people of each sort receive pleasure from what is naturally suited to them, owing to which the competitors before an audience of this sort must be allowed to employ some such kind of music as this); but for education, as has been said, the ethical class of melodies and of harmonies must be employed. And of that nature is the Dorian harmony, as we said before; but we must also accept any other harmony that those who take part in the pursuit of philosophy and in musical education may recommend to us. Socrates in the *Republic* does not do well in allowing only the Phrygian harmony along with the Dorian, and that when he has rejected the aulos among instruments; for the Phrygian harmony has the same effect among harmonies as the aulos among instruments—both are violently exciting and emotional. This is shown by poetry; for all Bacchic versification and all movement of that sort belong particularly to the aulos among the instruments, and these metres find their suitable accompaniment in melodies in the Phrygian harmony among the harmonies; for example the dithyramb is admittedly held to be a Phrygian metre, and the experts on this subject adduce many instances to prove this, particularly the fact that Philoxenus when he attempted to compose a dithyramb, "The Mysians," in the Dorian harmony was unable to do so, but merely by the force of nature fell back again into the suitable harmony, the Phrygian.[16] And all agree that the Dorian harmony is more sedate and of a specially manly character. Moreover since we praise and say that we ought to pursue the mean between extremes, and the Dorian harmony has this nature in relation to the other harmonies, it is clear that it suits the younger pupils to be educated rather in the Dorian melodies. But there are two objects to aim at, the possible as well as the suitable; for we are bound rather to attempt the things that are possible and those that are suitable for the particular class of people concerned; and in these matters also there are dividing lines drawn by the ages—for instance, those whose powers have waned through lapse of time cannot easily sing the intense harmonies, but to persons of that age nature suggests the relaxed

16 For the "Mysians," see J. F. Mountford in *Journal of Hellenic Studies*, XL (1920), 21-22.

harmonies. Therefore some musical experts also rightly criticize Socrates because he disapproved of the relaxed harmonies for amusement, taking them to have the character of intoxication, not in the sense of the effect of strong drink, for that clearly has more the result of making men frenzied revellers, but as failing in power. Hence even with a view to the period of life that is to follow, that of the comparatively old, it is proper to engage in the harmonies and melodies of this kind too, and also any kind of harmony that is suited to the age of boyhood because it is capable of being at once decorous and educative, which seems to be the nature of the Lydian most of all the harmonies. It is clear therefore that we should lay down these three canons to guide education—moderation, possibility, and suitability.

3. Aristoxenus

A pupil of the Pythagoreans and later of Aristotle, born about 350 B.C. at Tarentum in southern Italy, Aristoxenus is the most important of the ancient Greek writers about music. Of his numerous works only two books of the *Harmonic Elements* and fragments of the *Elements of Rhythmics* have come down to us. Aristoxenus' thought has a distinct empirical tendency. For example, he clearly perceives that listening to a musical composition presupposes an activity of collecting and building up impressions in one's memory. Aristoxenus also holds that the notes of a scale are to be judged, not by mathematical ratio, but by the ear. This empirical turn of mind makes Aristoxenus the first ancient writer to lay the foundation for a scientific aesthetics of music.

From the Harmonic Elements [1]

IT WILL be well perhaps to review in anticipation the course of our study; thus a foreknowledge of the road that we must travel will enable us to recognize each stage as we reach it, and so lighten the toil of the journey; nor shall we be harboring unknown to ourselves a false conception of our subject. Such was the condition, as Aristotle used often to relate, of most of the audience that attended Plato's lectures on the Good. They came, he used to say, every one of them, in the conviction that they would get from the lectures some one or other of the things that the world calls good; riches or health, or strength, in fine, some extraordinary gift of fortune. But when they found that Plato's reasonings were of sciences and numbers, and geometry, and astronomy, and of good and unity as predicates of the finite, methinks their disenchantment was complete. The result was that some of them sneered at the thing, while others vilified it. Now to what was all this trouble due? To the fact that they had not waited

1 Text: *The Harmonics of Aristoxenus,* as translated by H. S. Macran for the Clarendon Press (Oxford, 1902), pp. 187–198. Departures from Macran's wording are indicated by italics.

to inform themselves of the nature of the subject, but after the manner of the sect of word-catchers had flocked round open-mouthed, attracted by the mere title "good" in itself.

But if a general exposition of the subject had been given in advance, the intending pupil would either have abandoned his intention or if he was pleased with the exposition, would have remained in the said conviction to the end. It was for these very reasons, as he told us, that Aristotle himself used to give his intending pupils a preparatory statement of the subject and method of his course of study. And we agree with him in thinking, as we said at the beginning, that such prior information is desirable. For mistakes are often made in both directions. Some consider *harmonics* a sublime science, and expect a course of it to make them musicians; nay some even conceive it will exalt their moral nature. This mistake is due to their having run away with such phrases in our preamble as "we aim at the construction of every style of melody," and with our general statement "one class of musical art is hurtful to the moral character, another improves it"; while they missed completely our qualification of this statement, "in so far as musical art can improve the moral character." Then on the other hand there are persons who regard *harmonics* as quite a thing of no importance, and actually prefer to remain totally unacquainted even with its nature and aim. Neither of these views is correct. On the one hand the science is no proper object of contempt to the man of intelligence— this we shall see as the discussion progresses; nor on the other hand has it the quality of all-sufficiency, as some imagine. To be a musician, as we are always insisting, implies much more than a knowledge of *harmonics*, which is only one part of the musician's equipment, on the same level as the sciences of *rhythmics*, of *metrics*, of *organics*.

We shall now proceed to the consideration of *harmonics* and its parts. It is to be observed that in general the subject of our study is the question, In melody of every kind what are the natural laws according to which the voice in ascending or descending places the intervals? For we hold that the voice follows a natural law in its motion, and does not place the intervals at random. And of our answers we endeavor to supply proofs that will be in agreement with the phenomena—in this unlike our predecessors. For some of these introduced extraneous reasoning, and rejecting the senses as inaccurate, fabricated rational principles, asserting that height and depth of pitch consist in certain numerical ratios and relative rates of vibration—a theory utterly extraneous to the subject and quite at variance with the phenomena; while others, dispensing with reason and demonstration, confined themselves to isolated dogmatic statements, not being successful either in their enumeration of the mere phenomena. It is our endeavor that the principles which we assume shall without exception be evident to those who understand music, and that we shall advance to our conclusions by strict demonstration.

Our subject-matter then being all melody, whether vocal or instrumental, our method rests in the last resort on an appeal to the two faculties of hearing and intellect. By the former we judge the magnitudes of the intervals, by the latter we contemplate the functions of the notes. We must therefore accustom ourselves to an accurate discrimination of particulars. It is usual in geometrical constructions to use such a phrase as "Let this be a straight line"; but one must not be content with such language of assumption in the case of intervals. The geometrician makes no use of his faculty of sense-perception. He does not in any degree train his sight to discriminate the straight line, the circle, or any other figure, such training belonging rather to the practice of the carpenter, the turner, or some other such handicraftsman. But for the student of musical science accuracy of sense-perception is a fundamental requirement. For if his sense-perception is deficient, it is impossible for him to deal successfully with those questions that lie outside the sphere of sense-perception altogether. This will become clear in the course of our investigation. And we must bear in mind that musical cognition implies the simultaneous cognition of a permanent and of a changeable element, and that this applies without limitation or qualification to every branch of music. To begin with, our perception of the differences of the genera is dependent on the permanence of the containing, and the variation of the intermediate notes. Again, while the magnitude remains constant, we distinguish the interval between hypate and mese from that between paramese and nete; here, then, the magnitude is permanent, while the functions of the notes change; similarly, when there are several figures of the same magnitude, as of the *diatessaron*, or *diapente*, or any other; similarly, when the same interval leads or does not lead to modulation, according to its position. Again, in matters of rhythm we find many similar examples. Without any change in the characteristic proportion constituting any one genus of rhythm, the lengths of the feet vary in obedience to the general rate of movement; and while the magnitudes are constant, the quality of the feet undergoes a change; and the same magnitude serves as a foot and as a combination of feet. Plainly, too, unless there was a permanent quantum to deal with there could be no distinctions as to the methods of dividing it and arranging its parts. And in general, while rhythmical composition employs a rich variety of movements, the movements of the feet by which we note the rhythms are always simple and the same. Such, then, being the nature of music, we must in matters of harmony also accustom both ear and intellect to a correct judgment of the permanent and changeable element alike.

These remarks have exhibited the general character of the science called *harmonics*; and of this science there are, as a fact, seven parts.[2] Of these one and the first is to define the genera, and to show what are the permanent and what are the changeable elements presupposed by this distinction. None of our predecessors has drawn this distinction at all; nor is this to be wondered at. For they confined their attention to the enharmonic genus, to the neglect of the other two. Students of instruments, it is true, could not fail to distinguish each genus by ear, but none of them reflected even on the question, At what point does the enharmonic begin to pass into the chromatic? For their ability to discriminate each genus extended not to all the shades, inasmuch as they were not acquainted with all styles of musical composition or trained to exercise a nice discrimination in such distinctions; nor did they even observe that there were certain loci of the notes that alter their position with the change of genus. These reasons sufficiently explain why the genera have not as yet been definitely distinguished; but it is evident that we must supply this deficiency if we are to follow the differences that present themselves in works of musical composition.

Such is the first branch of *harmonics*. In the second we shall deal with intervals, omitting, to the best of our ability, none of the distinctions to be found in them. The majority of these, one might say, have as yet escaped observation. But we must bear in mind that wherever we come upon a distinction which has been overlooked, and not scientifically considered, we shall there fail to recognize the distinctions in works of melodic composition.

Again, since intervals are not in themselves sufficient to distinguish notes—for every magnitude, without qualification, that an interval can possess is common to several musical functions—the third part of our science will deal with notes, their number, and the means of recognizing them; and will consider the question whether they are certain points of pitch, as is vulgarly supposed, or whether they are musical functions, and also what is the meaning of a musical "function." Not one of these questions is clearly conceived by students of the subject.

The fourth part will consider *systems*, firstly as to their number and

---

2 In another order, the seven parts of harmonics are discussed at greater length by Cleonides in the selection that follows.

nature, secondly as to the manner of their construction from intervals and notes. Our predecessors have not regarded this part of the subject in either of these respects. On the one hand, no attention has been devoted to the questions whether intervals are collocated in any order to produce *systems*, or whether some collocations may not transgress a natural law. On the other hand, the distinctions in *systems* have not been completely enumerated by any of them. As to the first point, our forerunners simply ignored the distinction between "melodious" and "unmelodious"; as to the second, they either made no attempt at all at enumeration of *system-distinctions*, confining their attention to the seven *octachords* which they called harmonies; or if they made the attempt, they fell very short of completeness, like the school of Pythagoras of Zacynthus, and Agenor of Mitylene. The order that distinguishes the melodious from the unmelodious resembles that which we find in the collocation of letters in language. For it is not every collocation but only certain collocations of any given letters that will produce a syllable.

The fifth part of our science deals with the *tones* in which the *systems* are placed for the purposes of melody. No explanation has yet been offered of the manner in which those *tones* are to be found, or of the principle by which one must be guided in enunciating their number. The account of the *tones* given by the harmonists closely resembles the observance of the days according to which, for example, the tenth day of the month at Corinth is the fifth at Athens, and the eighth somewhere else. Just in the same way, some of the harmonists hold that the Hypodorian is the lowest of the *tones;* that a *semitone* above lies the Mixolydian; a *semitone* higher again the Dorian; a tone above the Dorian the Phrygian; likewise a tone above the Phrygian the Lydian. The number is sometimes increased by the addition of the Hypophrygian [3] at the bottom of the list. Others, again, having regard to the boring of finger-holes on the *auloi*, assume intervals of three *dieses* between the three lowest *tones*, the Hypophrygian, the Hypodorian, and the Dorian; a tone between the Dorian and Phrygian; three *dieses* again between the Phrygian and Lydian, and the same distance between the Lydian and Mixolydian. But they have not informed us on what principle they have persuaded themselves to this location of the *tones*. And that the close packing of small intervals is unmelodious and of no practical value whatsoever will be clear in the course of our discussion.

Again, since some melodies are simple, and others contain a modulation,

---

3 At the suggestion of my friend Whitney J. Oates of Princeton University, I omit the word "aulos," which seems not to belong in the text.

we must treat of modulation, considering first the nature of modulation in the abstract, and how it arises, or in other words, to what modification in the melodic order it owes its existence; secondly, how many modulations there are in all, and at what intervals they occur. On these questions we find no statements by our predecessors with or without proof.

The last section of our science is concerned with the actual *composition* of melody. For since in the same notes, indifferent in themselves, we have the choice of numerous melodic forms of every character, it is evident that here we have the practical question of the employment of the notes; and this is what we mean by the *composition* of melody. The science of harmony having traversed the said sections will find its consummation here.

It is plain that the apprehension of a melody consists in noting with both ear and intellect every distinction as it arises in the successive sounds —successive, for melody, like all branches of music, consists in a successive production. For the apprehension of music depends on these two faculties, sense-perception and memory; for we must perceive the sound that is present, and remember that which is past. In no other way can we follow the phenomena of music.

Now some find the goal of the science called *harmonics* in the notation of melodies, declaring this to be the ultimate limit of the apprehension of any given melody. Others again find it in the knowledge of the *auloi*, and in the ability to tell the manner of production of, and the agencies employed in, any piece rendered on the *aulos*.

Such views are conclusive evidence of an utter misconception. So far is notation from being the perfection of harmonic science that it is not even a part of it, any more than the marking of any particular metre is a part of metrical science. As in the latter case one might very well mark the scheme of the iambic metre without understanding its essence, so it is with melody also; if a man notes down the Phrygian scale it does not follow that he must know the essence of the Phrygian scale. Plainly then notation is not the ultimate limit of our science.

That the premises of our argument are true, and that the faculty of musical notation argues nothing beyond a discernment of the size of intervals, will be clear on consideration. In the use of signs for the intervals no peculiar mark is employed to denote all their individual distinctions, such as the several methods of dividing the *diatessaron*, which depend on the differences of genera, or of the several figures of the same interval which result from a variation in the disposition of the simple intervals. It is the same with the musical functions proper to the natures of the different tetrachords; the same notation is employed for the tetrachords hyperbolaion, neton, meson, and hypaton. Thus the signs fail to distinguish the functional differences, and consequently indicate the magnitudes of the intervals, and nothing more. But that the mere sense-discrimination of magnitudes is no part of the general comprehension of music was stated in the introduction, and the following considerations will make it patent. Mere knowledge of magnitudes does not enlighten one as to the functions of the tetrachords, or of the notes, or the differences of the genera or, briefly, the difference of *incomposite* and *composite* intervals, or the distinction between modulating and non-modulating *systems,* or the *styles* of melodic *composition,* or indeed anything else of the kind.

Now if the harmonists, as they are called, have in their ignorance seriously entertained this view, while there is nothing preposterous in their motives, their ignorance must be profound and invincible. But if, being aware that notation is not the final goal of *harmonics,* they have propounded this view merely through the desire to please amateurs, and to represent as the perfection of the science a certain visible activity, their motives deserve condemnation as very preposterous indeed. In the first place they would constitute the amateur judge of the sciences—and it is preposterous that the same person should be learner and judge of the same thing; in the second place they reverse the proper order in their fancy of representing a visible activity as the consummation of intellectual apprehension; for, as a fact, the ultimate factor in every visible activity is the intellectual process. For this latter is the presiding and determining principle; and as for the hands, voice, mouth, or breath—it is an error to suppose that they are very much more than inanimate instruments. And if this intellectual activity is something hidden deep down in the soul, and is not palpable or apparent to the ordinary man, as the operations of the hand and the like are apparent, we must not on that account alter our views. We shall be sure to miss the truth unless we place the supreme and ultimate, not in the thing determined, but in the activity that determines.

No less preposterous is the above-mentioned theory concerning the *auloi.* Nay, rather there is no error so fatal and so preposterous as to base the natural laws of harmony on any instrument. The essence and order of harmony depend not upon any of the properties of instruments. It is not because the *aulos* has finger-holes and bores, and the like, nor is it because it submits to certain operations of the hands and of the other parts naturally adapted to raise and lower the pitch, that the *diatessaron,* and the *diapente,* and the *diapason* are *symphonies,* or that each of the other intervals possesses its proper magnitude. For even with all these conditions present, players on the *aulos* fail for the most part to attain the exact order of melody; and whatever small success attends them is due to the employment of agencies external to the instrument, as in the well-known expedients of drawing the two *auloi* apart, and bringing them alongside, and of raising and lowering the pitch by changing the pressure of the breath. Plainly, then, one is as much justified in attributing their failures as their success to the essential nature of the *aulos*. But this would not have been so if there was anything gained by basing harmony on the nature of an instrument. In that case, as an immediate consequence of tracing melody up to its original in the nature of the *aulos*, we should have found it there fixed, unerring, and correct. But as a fact neither the *auloi* nor any other instrument will supply a foundation for the principles of harmony. There is a certain marvellous order which belongs to the nature of harmony in general; in this order every instrument, to the best of its ability, participates under the direction of that faculty of sense-perception on which they, as well as everything else in music, finally depend. To suppose, because one sees day by day the finger-holes the same and the strings at the same tension, that one will find in these harmony with its permanence and eternally immutable order—this is sheer folly. For as there is no harmony in the strings save that which the cunning of the hand confers upon them, so is there none in the finger-holes save what has been introduced by the same agency. That no instrument is self-tuned, and that the harmonizing of it is the prerogative of the sense-perception is obvious, and requires no proof. It is strange that the supporters of this absurd theory can cling to it in face of the fact that the *auloi* are perpetually in a state of change; and of course what is played on the instrument varies with the variation in the agencies employed in its production. It is surely clear then that on no consideration can melody be based on the *auloi*; for, firstly, an instrument will not supply a foundation for the order of harmony, and secondly, even if it were supposed that harmony should be based on some instrument, the choice should not have fallen on the *aulos*, an instrument especially liable to aberrations, resulting from the manufacture and manipulation of it, and from its own peculiar nature.

This will suffice as an introductory account of harmonic science; but as we prepare ourselves to enter upon the study of the *Elements* we must at the outset attend to the following considerations. Our exposition cannot be a successful one unless three conditions be fulfilled. Firstly, the phenomena themselves must be correctly observed; secondly, what is prior and what is derivative in them must be properly discriminated; thirdly, our conclusions and inferences must follow legitimately from the premises. And as in every science that consists of several propositions the proper course is to find certain principles from which to deduce the dependent truths, we must be guided in our selection of principles by two considerations. Firstly, every proposition that is to serve as a principle must be true and evident; secondly, it must be such as to be accepted by the sense-perception as one of the primary truths of harmonic science. For what requires demonstration cannot stand as a fundamental principle; and in general we must be watchful in determining our highest principles, lest on the one hand we let ourselves be dragged outside the proper track of our science by beginning with sound in general regarded as air-vibration, or on the other hand turn short of the flag and abandon much of what truly belongs to *harmonics*.

4. Cleonides

Of Cleonides we know only that several early manuscripts name him as the author of the little treatise that follows. From his account of the keys, in which there is no mention of Hyperaeolian and Hyperlydian, his French translator Ruelle concludes that he must have lived before the time of Alypius and Aristides Quintilianus (1st century A.D.), the earliest writers to speak of these additions to the Aristoxenian system. Actually, this would seem to suggest just the opposite. As an abbreviator and popularizer of Aristoxenus, Cleonides has no reason to mention these additions; the significant thing is that in naming the keys he uses both the Aristoxenian and the later nomenclature. Since the later nomenclature is patently devised for the extended system of fifteen keys, he must have lived after the time when this system was introduced. For the rest, he adheres so closely to Aristoxenus, even in his terminology and wording, that his little abstract is in effect a compensation for the loss of that part of the Aristoxenian writing which has not been preserved. This is in itself enough to dispose of the attribution to Euclid, found in many of the sources, for the teachings of Aristoxenus and of Euclid, in his *Division of the Canon*, are diametrically opposed. In a Latin translation by Georgius Valla, the *Eisagoge* of Cleonides was printed in Venice as early as 1497. It thus became one of the sources from which the musicians of the Renaissance drew their information about the music of Classical Antiquity.

Harmonic Introduction [1]

1. HARMONICS is the speculative and practical science having to do with the nature of the harmonious. And the harmonious is what is made up of notes and intervals having a certain order. The parts of harmonics are

---

1 Text: Karl von Jan, *Musici Scriptores Graeci* (Leipzig, 1895), pp. 179–207. There is a French translation by C. E. Ruelle (Paris, 1884).

seven: it has to do with notes, intervals, genera, systems (or scales), tones (or keys), modulations, and melodic composition.

A note is a harmonious incidence of the voice upon a single pitch.

An interval is what is bounded by two notes differing as to height and depth.

Genus is a certain division of four notes.

A system is what is made up of more than one interval.

A tone is any region of the voice, apt for the reception of a system; it is without breadth.

Modulation is the transposition of a similar thing to a dissimilar region.

Melodic composition is the employment of the materials subject to harmonic practice with due regard to the requirements of each of the subjects under consideration.

2. The things considered under quality of voice are these. It has two sorts of movements: one is called continuous and belongs to speech, the other is diastematic and belongs to melody. In continuous movement, tensions and relaxations occur imperceptibly and the voice is never at rest until it becomes silent. In diastematic movement, the opposite takes place; the voice dwells on certain points and passes over the distances between them, proceeding first in the one way, then in the other. The points on which it dwells we call pitches, the passages from pitch to pitch we call intervals. The causes of the difference between pitches are tension and relaxation, their effects are height and depth. For the result of tension is to lead toward the high, that of relaxation toward the low. And height is the effect resulting from tension, depth that resulting from relaxation. Pitches are also called notes: one calls them "pitches" (τάσεις) when they are produced by instruments that are struck, because of their being stretched (τετάσθαι); one calls them "notes" (φθόγγοι) when they are produced by the voice. For to be stretched is a property of both. Considered as pitches, the number of notes is infinite; considered as functions, there are in each genus eighteen.

3. The genera are three: diatonic, chromatic, and enharmonic. The diatonic is sung in descending by tone, tone, and semitone, but in ascending by semitone, tone, and tone. The chromatic is sung in descending by trihemitone, semitone, and semitone, but in ascending by semitone, semitone, and trihemitone. The enharmonic is sung in descending by ditone, diesis, and diesis, but in ascending by diesis, diesis, and ditone.

4. In the diatonic, chromatic, and enharmonic genera the notes are these:

Proslambanomenos	Proslambanomenos	Proslambanomenos
Hypate hypaton	Hypate hypaton	Hypate hypaton
Parhypate hypaton	Parhypate hypaton	Parhypate hypaton
Diatonic lichanos hypaton	Chromatic lichanos hypaton	Enharmonic lichanos hypaton
Hypate meson	Hypate meson	Hypate meson
Parhypate meson	Parhypate meson	Parhypate meson
Diatonic lichanos meson	Chromatic lichanos meson	Enharmonic lichanos meson
Mese	Mese	Mese
Trite synemmenon	Trite synemmenon	Trite synemmenon
Diatonic paranete synemmenon	Chromatic paranete synemmenon	Enharmonic paranete synemmenon
Nete synemmenon	Nete synemmenon	Nete synemmenon
Paramese	Paramese	Paramese
Trite diezeugmenon	Trite diezeugmenon	Trite diezeugmenon
Diatonic paranete diezeugmenon	Chromatic paranete diezeugmenon	Enharmonic paranete diezeugmenon
Nete diezeugmenon	Nete diezeugmenon	Nete diezeugmenon
Trite hyperbolaion	Trite hyperbolaion	Trite hyperbolaion
Diatonic paranete hyperbolaion	Chromatic paranete hyperbolaion	Enharmonic paranete hyperbolaion
Nete hyperbolaion	Nete hyperbolaion	Nete hyperbolaion

In the blending of the genera they are these:

Proslambanomenos

Hypate hypaton
Parhypate hypaton
Enharmonic lichanos hypaton
Chromatic lichanos hypaton
Diatonic lichanos hypaton

Hypate meson
Parhypate meson
Enharmonic lichanos meson
Chromatic lichanos meson
Diatonic lichanos meson
Mese

Trite synemmenon
Enharmonic paranete synemmenon

Chromatic paranete synemmenon
Diatonic paranete synemmenon
Nete synemmenon

Paramese
Trite diezeugmenon
Enharmonic paranete diezeugmenon
Chromatic paranete diezeugmenon
Diatonic paranete diezeugmenon
Nete diezeugmenon

Trite hyperbolaion
Enharmonic paranete hyperbolaion
Chromatic paranete hyperbolaion
Diatonic paranete hyperbolaion
Nete hyperbolaion

Of the notes enumerated some are fixed, others movable. The fixed notes are all those that remain unchanged and on the same pitches in the different genera. The movable notes are all those in the opposite case; these do not remain unchanged and on the same pitches in the different genera. The fixed notes are eight, namely the proslambanomenos, hypate hypaton, hypate meson, mese, nete synemmenon, paramese, nete diezeugmenon, and nete hyperbolaion; the movable notes are all those that lie between these.

Of the fixed notes some are barypykna, others lie outside the pykna and bound the perfect systems. Five are barypykna, namely the hypate hypaton, hypate meson, mese, paramese, and nete diezeugmenon. The other three lie outside the pykna and bound the perfect systems, namely the proslambanomenos, nete synemmenon, and nete hyperbolaion.

Of the movable notes some are mesopykna, others are oxypykna, others are diatonic. Five are mesopykna, namely the parhypate hypaton, parhypate meson, trite synemmenon, trite diezeugmenon, and trite hyperbolaion. In each genus five are oxypykna: in the enharmonic genus of enharmonic pykna, in the chromatic genus of chromatic pykna; the diatonic genus does not share in the pyknon. In the enharmonic they are these: the enharmonic lichanos hypaton, enharmonic lichanos meson, enharmonic paranete synemmenon, enharmonic paranete diezeugmenon, and enharmonic paranete hyperbolaion. In the chromatic they are these: the chromatic lichanos hypaton, chromatic lichanos meson, chromatic paranete synemmenon, chromatic paranete diezeugmenon, and chromatic paranete hyperbolaion. In the diatonic they are these: the diatonic lichanos hypaton, diatonic lichanos meson, diatonic paranete synemmenon, diatonic paranete diezeugmenon, and diatonic paranete hyperbolaion.

5. Of intervals the differences are five, in that they differ from one another in magnitude, and in genus, and as the symphonic from the diaphonic, and as the composite from the incomposite, and as the rational from the irrational. They differ in magnitude in so far as some intervals are larger and others smaller, for example the ditone, tone, semitone, diatessaron, diapente, diapason, and the like. They differ in genus in so far as some intervals are diatonic, others chromatic, and others enharmonic. They differ as the symphonic from the diaphonic in so far as some intervals are symphonic and others diaphonic. The symphonic intervals are the diatessaron, diapente, diapason, and the like. The diaphonic intervals are all those smaller than the diatessaron and all those lying between the symphonic intervals. The intervals smaller than the diatessaron are the diesis, semitone, tone, trihemitone, and ditone; those lying between the symphonic intervals are the tritone, the tetratone, the pentatone, and the like. And symphony is a blending of two notes, a higher and a lower; diaphony, on the contrary, is a refusal of two notes to combine, with the result that they do not blend but grate harshly on the ear. Intervals differ in composition in so far as some are incomposite and others composite. The incomposite intervals are those bounded by consecutive notes, for example the intervals bounded by the hypate and parhypate and by the lichanos and mese; the same applies to the remaining intervals. The composite intervals are those not bounded by consecutive notes, for example the intervals bounded by the mese and parhypate and by the mese and nete and by the paramese and hypate. Thus certain intervals are common to the composite and incomposite, namely those from the semitone to the ditone. For the semitone is composite in the enharmonic genus, but incomposite in the chromatic and diatonic; the tone is composite in the chromatic genus, but incomposite in the diatonic; the trihemitone is incomposite in the chromatic genus, but composite in the diatonic; the ditone is incomposite in the enharmonic genus, but composite in the chromatic and diatonic. All intervals smaller than the semitone are incomposite; all intervals larger than the ditone are composite. Intervals differ as the rational from the irrational in so far as some are rational and others irrational. The rational intervals are those whose magnitudes can be defined, such as the tone, semitone, ditone, tritone, and the like. The irrational intervals are those deviating from these magnitudes to a greater or lesser degree by some irrational quantity.

6. The genera are the three already enumerated. For every melody

will be either diatonic or chromatic or enharmonic or common or a mixture of these. The diatonic genus is the one using diatonic division, the chromatic genus the one using chromatic division, the enharmonic genus the one using enharmonic division. The common genus is the one made up of the fixed notes. The mixed genus is the one in which two or three generic characteristics reveal themselves, such as diatonic and chromatic, or diatonic and enharmonic, or chromatic and enharmonic, or diatonic, chromatic, and enharmonic. The differences of the genera arise in connection with the movable notes, for the lichanos is moved within the locus of a tone, the parhypate within that of a diesis. Thus the highest lichanos is that a tone distant from the upper boundary of the tetrachord, the lowest that a ditone distant. In the same way the lowest parhypate is a diesis distant from the lower boundary of the tetrachord, the highest a semitone distant.

7. Shade is a specific division of a genus. There are six distinct and recognized shades: one enharmonic, three chromatic, and two diatonic.

The shade of the enharmonic uses the division of the genus itself, for it is sung by a diesis equivalent to a quarter-tone, another diesis equal to it, and a ditone.

Of the chromatic divisions, the lowest is the shade of the soft chromatic; it is sung by a diesis equivalent to a third-tone, another diesis equal to it, and the equivalent of a tone plus a half-tone plus a third-tone. The hemiolic chromatic is sung by a hemiolic diesis equivalent to one and one-half times the enharmonic diesis, another diesis equal to it, and an incomposite interval equivalent to seven enharmonic dieses. The tonic chromatic uses the shade of the genus itself, for it is sung by semitone, semitone, and trihemitone. And the chromatic shades just enumerated take their names from their pykna: the tonic chromatic from the tone inherent in its pyknon as a composite interval; the hemiolic chromatic from the hemiolic diesis inherent in its pyknon, one and one-half times the enharmonic diesis; in the same way the soft chromatic is the one having the least pyknon, seeing that its pyknon is relaxed and tuned down.

Of the diatonic divisions one is called soft, the other syntonic. The shade of the soft diatonic is sung by a semitone, an incomposite interval equivalent to three enharmonic dieses, and an interval equivalent to five enharmonic dieses, likewise incomposite. That of the syntonic diatonic shares the division of the genus itself, for it is sung by semitone, tone, and tone.

The shades are also shown by numbers in this manner. The tone is assumed to be divided into twelve least parts, of which each one is called a twelfth-tone. The remaining intervals are also assumed to be divided in

the same proportion, the semitone into six twelfths, the diesis equivalent
to a quarter-tone into three twelfths, the diesis equivalent to a third-tone
into four twelfths, the whole diatessaron into thirty twelfths. In terms
of quantity, then, the enharmonic will be sung by 3, 3, and 24 twelfths, the
soft chromatic by 4, 4, and 22, the hemiolic chromatic by 4½, 4½ and
21, the tonic chromatic by 6, 6, and 18, the soft diatonic by 6, 9, and 15,
the syntonic diatonic by 6, 12, and 12.

8. Of systems the differences are seven. Four of these were found also
in intervals; these are the differences in magnitude, in genus, of the symphonic and diaphonic, and of the rational and irrational. Three differences
are peculiar to systems; these are the differences of the progression by
step and by leap, of the conjunct and the disjunct, and of the non-modulating and the modulating. In magnitude the larger systems differ from the
smaller, as the system of the diapason from that of the tritone or diapente
or diatessaron or the like. In genus the diatonic systems differ from the
enharmonic or chromatic, or the chromatic or enharmonic from the others.
Considered as symphonic or diaphonic, the systems bounded by symphonies will differ from those bounded by diaphonies. Of the systems
within the non-modulating system six are symphonic: the smallest is
that of the diatessaron, of two tones and a half, for example that from
the hypate hypaton to hypate meson; the second, that of the diapente,
of three tones and a half, for example that from the proslambanomenos
to hypate meson; the third, that of the diapason, of six tones, for
example that from the proslambanomenos to mese; the fourth, that
of the diapason plus diatessaron, of eight tones and a half, for example that from the proslambanomenos to nete synemmenon or diatonic
paranete diezeugmenon; the fifth, that of the diapason plus diapente, of
nine tones and a half, for example that from the proslambanomenos to
nete diezeugmenon; the sixth, that of the double diapason, of twelve
tones, for example that from the proslambanomenos to nete hyperbolaion.
The synemmenon system goes only as far as the fourth symphony; in this
system the first symphony is that of the diatessaron, the second that of the
diapente, the third that of the diapason, the fourth that of the diapason
plus diatessaron. But the region of the voice extends to the seventh and
eighth symphonies, which are the double diapason plus diatessaron and
the double diapason plus diapente. The diaphonic systems are those
smaller than that of the diatessaron and all those lying between the
symphonic systems.

9. Figures (or species) of a particular magnitude arise when the order
of the simple parts of the given whole undergoes a change with respect to

some dissimilar constituent part, the magnitude and number of the parts remaining the same. For when the parts are all equal and similar there is no change in the figures.[2]

Of the diatessaron there are three species. The first is that bounded by barypykna, as is that from the hypate hypaton to hypate meson; the second that bounded by mesopykna, as is that from the parhypate hypaton to parhypate meson; the third that bounded by oxypykna, as is that from the lichanos hypaton to lichanos meson. Thus in the enharmonic and chromatic genera the figures are comprehended in accordance with the nature of the pyknon.

But in the diatonic genus the figures do not occur in connection with a pyknon, for this genus is divided into semitones and tones. The symphony of the diatessaron contains one semitone and two tones; in the same way the diapente contains one semitone and three tones and the diapason two semitones and five tones. In this genus, then, the figures are considered in accordance with the nature of the semitones. Thus in the diatonic genus the first species of the diatessaron is that in which the semitone lies below the tones, the second that in which it lies above the tones, the third that in which it lies between the tones. And these species begin and end with the same notes as in the other genera.

Of the diapente there are four figures. The first, bounded by barypykna, is that in which the tone is at the top; it extends from the hypate meson to paramese. The second, bounded by mesopykna, is that in which the tone is second from the top; it extends from the parhypate meson to trite diezeugmenon. The third, bounded by oxypykna, is that in which the tone is third from the top; it extends from the lichanos meson to paranete diezeugmenon. The fourth, bounded by barypykna, is that in which the tone is at the bottom; it extends from the mese to nete diezeugmenon or from the proslambanomenos to hypate meson.

In the diatonic genus the first figure is that in which the semitone lies at the bottom, the second that in which it lies at the top, the third that in which it is second from the top, the fourth that in which it is third from the top.

Of the diapason there are seven species. The first, bounded by barypykna, is that in which the tone is at the top; it extends from the hypate hypaton to paramese and was called Mixolydian by the ancients.

---

2 Cf. Aristoxenus, *Harmonic Elements* (Macran's edition, p. 222): "Such a difference [of species] arises when the order of the simple parts of a certain whole is altered, while both the number and magnitude of those parts remain the same": also Aristotle, *Politics*, 1276B: "And similarly with any other common whole or composite structure we say it is different if the form (εἶδος) of its composition is different—for instance a harmony consisting of the same notes we call different if at one time it is Dorian and at another Phrygian." [Rackham]

The second, bounded by mesopykna, is that in which the tone is second from the top; it extends from the parhypate hypaton to trite diezeugmenon and was called Lydian.

The third, bounded by oxypykna, is that in which the tone is third from the top; it extends from the lichanos hypaton to paranete diezeugmenon and was called Phrygian.

The fourth, bounded by barypykna, is that in which the tone is fourth from the top; it extends from the hypate meson to nete diezeugmenon and was called Dorian.

The fifth, bounded by mesopykna, is that in which the tone is fifth from the top; it extends from the parhypate meson to trite hyperbolaion and was called Hypolydian.

The sixth, bounded by oxypykna, is that in which the tone is sixth from the top; it extends from the lichanos meson to paranete hyperbolaion and was called Hypophrygian.

The seventh, bounded by barypykna, is that in which the tone is at the bottom; it extends from the mese to nete hyperbolaion or from the proslambanomenos to mese and was called common or Locrian or Hypodorian.

In the diatonic genus the first species of the diapason is that in which the semitone is first from the bottom but fourth from the top; the second is that in which it is third from the bottom but first from the top; the third is that in which it is second from either end; the fourth is that in which it is first from the bottom but third from the top; the fifth is that in which it is fourth from the bottom but first from the top; the sixth is that in which it is third from the bottom but second from the top; the seventh is that in which it is second from the bottom but third from the top. And these species begin and end with the same notes as in the enharmonic and chromatic genera and were called by the same names.

Considered as rational and irrational, the systems made up of rational intervals will differ from those made up of irrational ones, for those made up of rational intervals are rational, those made up of irrational ones irrational.

Considered as progressing by step and by leap, the systems that are sung by consecutive notes will differ from those that are sung by notes that are not consecutive.

Considered as conjunct and disjunct, the systems put together from conjunct tetrachords will differ from those put together from disjunct. And a conjunction is the note common to two tetrachords of the same species, sung one after another; a disjunction is the tone between two tetrachords of the same species, sung one after another. There are in all three conjunctions: the middle, the highest, and the lowest. The lowest conjunction is that of the tetrachords hypate and meson; the note common to this conjunction is the hypate meson. The middle conjunction is that of the tetrachords meson and neton synemmenon; the note common to this conjunction is the mese. The highest conjunction is that of the tetrachords neton diezeugmenon and hyperbolaion; the note common to this conjunction is the nete diezeugmenon. There is one disjunction, that of the tetrachords meson and neton diezeugmenon; the tone common to this disjunction is that from the mese to paramese.

Of perfect systems there are two, of which one is lesser, the other greater. The Lesser Perfect System is that by conjunction, extending from the proslambanomenos to nete synemmenon. There are in this system three conjunct tetrachords, namely the hypaton, meson, and synemmenon, and there is a tone between the proslambanomenos and hypate hypaton; this system is bounded by the symphony diapason plus diatessaron.

The Greater Perfect System is that by disjunction, extending from the proslambanomenos to nete hyperbolaion. There are in this system four tetrachords, two conjunct pairs mutually disjunct, namely the hypaton and meson and the diezeugmenon and hyperbolaion, and there are two tones, one between the proslambanomenos and hypate hypaton, the other between the mese and paramese; this system is bounded by the symphony double diapason.

Of the five tetrachords in the non-modulating system, which is put together from the two perfect ones, two are common to both the perfect systems: the tetrachords hypaton and meson; peculiar to the conjunct system is the tetrachord neton synemmenon; peculiar to the disjunct system are the tetrachords neton diezeugmenon and hyperbolaion.

11. Considered as non-modulating and modulating, the systems will differ in so far as the simple systems differ from those that are not simple. The simple systems are those in harmony with one mese, the duple those in harmony with two, the triple those in harmony with three, the multiple those in harmony with many. To be a mese is the function of the note whose property it is, in disjunction, to have above it an incomposite tone (this part of the system remaining unaffected) but below it an incomposite or composite ditone; in conjunction, however, there being three conjunct tetrachords, it is its property to be the highest note of the middle tetra-

chord or the lowest note of the highest tetrachord. And it is from the mese that the functions of the remaining notes are recognized, for it is clearly in relation to the mese that each of them is thus or thus.[3]

12. The word "tone" is used in four senses: as note, interval, region of the voice, and pitch. It is used in the sense of note in the epithet "seven-toned" as applied to the phorminx, for instance by Terpander and Ion. The former says:

To thee we will play new hymns upon a phorminx of seven tones and will love the four-voiced lay no more; [4]

the latter:

Eleven-stringèd lyre with thy flight of ten steps into the place where the three concordant roads of Harmonia meet, once all the Greeks raised but a meagre music, playing thee seven-toned four by four.[5]

And not a few others have used the epithet. We use the word "tone" in the sense of interval whenever we say that it is a tone from the mese to paramese.

We use it of the region of the voice whenever we speak of Dorian, or Phrygian, or Lydian, or any of the other tones. According to Aristoxenus there are 13 tones:

Hypermixolydian, also called Hyperphrygian;
Two Mixolydians, a higher and a lower, of which the higher is also called Hyperiastian, the lower Hyperdorian;
Two Lydians, a higher and a lower, of which the lower is also called Aeolian;
Two Phrygians, a higher and a lower, of which the lower is also called Iastian;
One Dorian;
Two Hypolydians, a higher and a lower, the latter also called Hypoaeolian;
Two Hypophrygians, of which the lower is also called Hypoiastian;
Hypodorian.

Of these the highest is the Hypermixolydian, the lowest the Hypodorian. From the highest to the lowest, the distance between consecutive tones is a semitone, between two parallel tones a trihemitone; with the distance between the remaining tones the case will be similar. The Hypermixolydian is a diapason above the Hypodorian.

3 On the function of the mese cf. Aristotle, *Metaphysics*, 1018B; *Politics*, 1254A; *Problems*, 1919A (Problem 20).
4 Translation by J. M. Edmonds; see his edition of the *Lyra Graeca* for the Loeb Classical Library, I (London, 1928), 33.

5 Translation by J. M. Edmonds; see his *Elegy and Iambus*, published in the Loeb Classical Library, I (London, 1931), 433.

We use the word "tone" in the sense of pitch when we speak of using a higher or lower or intermediate tone of voice.

13. The word "modulation" is used in four senses: with reference to genus, system, tone, and melodic composition. Modulation in genus takes place whenever there is a modulation from the diatonic genus to the chromatic or enharmonic, or from the chromatic or enharmonic to some one of the others. Modulation in system takes place whenever there is a modulation from the conjunct system to the disjunct, or vice versa. Modulation in tone takes place whenever there is a modulation from the Dorian tone to the Phrygian, or from the Phrygian to the Lydian or Hypermixolydian or Hypodorian, or in general whenever there is a modulation from any one of the thirteen tones to any other. Modulations begin with the semitone and proceed to the diapason, some of them being made by symphonic intervals, others by diaphonic. Those made by symphonic intervals and by that of the tone are melodious. Of the rest, some are more melodious than unmelodious, others less so. For the greater or less the community of elements, the more melodious or unmelodious the modulation, seeing that every modulation requires the presence of some common element, whether a note, an interval, or a system. But this community is determined by the similarity of the notes, for a modulation is melodious or unmelodious in so far as it involves the coincidence of notes that are similar or dissimilar with respect to their participation in a pyknon.

Modulation in melodic composition takes place whenever there is a modulation in ethos from the diastaltic to the systaltic or hesychastic, or from the hesychastic to some one of the others.[6] The diastaltic ethos in melodic composition is that which reveals heroic deeds and the grandeur and loftiness of a manly soul and an affection akin to these. It is most used in tragedy and in all things that border on this character. The systaltic ethos is that by which the soul is brought into dejection and an effeminate condition. Such a state will correspond to erotic affections and to dirges and expressions of pity and things resembling these. The hesychastic ethos is that which accompanies quietude of soul and a liberal and peaceful state. To it will correspond hymns, paeans, eulogies, counsels, and things similar to these.

14. Melodic composition is the use of the enumerated parts of harmonics, which have the function of subject-matter. Melodic composition is accomplished by means of four figures: succession, plexus or network, repetition or selection, and prolongation. Succession is a progression of the

---

6 Cf. the threefold classification of Aristotle, *Politics*, 1341B (p. 22 above).

melody by consecutive notes; plexus or network a placing of intervals side by side; repetition or selection a striking of a single tone, repeated several times; prolongation a dwelling for a greater time-interval on a single utterance of the voice.

5. Athenaeus

A Greek rhetorician and grammarian of Naucratis in Egypt, Athenaeus lived in Rome about 200 A.D. Of his works we still possess fifteen books of the *Deipnosophistai* (Sophists at Dinner)—originally thirty books—an immense mine of information on matters connected with everyday life, the table, music, songs, dances, games, literature, etc. Its value as source material cannot be overestimated, as it is filled with quotations from writers whose works have not been preserved. In all, Athenaeus refers to nearly 800 writers. The work professes to be an account given by the author to his friend Timocrates of a banquet held at the house of Laurentius, a scholar and wealthy patron of art.

From the Sophists at Dinner [1]

ON THE subject of music there was daily conversation, some saying things recorded here, others saying other things, but all joining in praise of this kind of amusement; and Masurius, in all things excellent and wise (for he is a jurist second to none, and he has always been devoted to music and has taken up the playing of musical instruments), said: The comic poet Eupolis, my friends, remarks: "Music is a matter deep and intricate," and it is always supplying something new for those who can perceive. Hence Anaxilas, also, says in *Hyacinthus:* "Music is like Libya, which, I swear by the gods, brings forth some new creature every year." To quote *The Harp-Singer* of Theophilus: "A mighty treasure, good sirs, and a constant one, is music for all who have learned it and are educated." For indeed it trains character, and tames the hot-tempered and those whose opinions clash. The Pythagorean Cleinias, for example, as Chamaeleon of Pontus records, whose conduct and character were exemplary,

1 Text: *The Deipnosophists*, VI (Cambridge, Mass., Harvard University Press, 1937), 361–387, 409–419. Translated for the Loeb Classical Library by Charles Burton Gulick. Reprinted by permission of Harvard University Press.

would always take his cithara and play on it whenever it happened that he was exasperated to the point of anger. And in answer to those who inquired the reason he would say, "I am calming myself down." So, too, the Homeric Achilles calmed himself with his cithara, which was the only thing Homer grants to him out of the booty taken from Eëtion, and which had the power of allaying his fiery nature. He, at least, is the only one in the *Iliad* who plays this kind of music. That music can also heal diseases Theophrastus has recorded in his work *On Inspiration:* he says that persons subject to sciatica would always be free from its attacks if one played the aulos in the Phrygian harmony over the part affected. This harmony was first discovered by the Phrygians and constantly used by them. For this reason, he says, aulos-players among the Greeks have names which are Phrygian and appropriate to slaves; such, for example, is Sambas, mentioned by Alcman, also Adon and Telus, and in Hipponax, Cion, Codalus, and Babys, who occasioned the proverb said of those whose aulos-playing grows ever worse and worse, "Babys is playing worse." Aristoxenus attributes its invention to the Phrygian Hyagnis.

Heracleides of Pontus, however, says in the third book of his work *On Music* that the Phrygian should not be called a separate harmony any more than the Lydian. For there are only three harmonies, since there are also only three kinds of Greeks—Dorians, Aeolians, and Ionians. There is no small difference in the characters of these three, for while the Lacedaemonians preserve better than all other Dorians the customs of their fathers, and the Thessalians (these are they who conferred upon the Aeolians the origin of their race) have always maintained practically the same mode of life, the great majority of the Ionians, on the other hand, have undergone changes due to barbarian rulers who have for the time being come in contact with them. Hence the melodic style which the Dorians constructed they called the Dorian harmony; Aeolian they called the harmony which the Aeolians sang; Ionian, they said of the third one, which they heard Ionians sing. Now the Dorian harmony exhibits the quality of manly vigor, of magnificent bearing, not relaxed or merry, but sober and intense, neither varied nor complicated. But the Aeolian character contains the elements of ostentation and turgidity, and even conceit; these qualities are in keeping with their horse-breeding and their way of meeting strangers; yet this does not mean malice, but is, rather, lofty and confident. Hence also their fondness for drinking is something appropriate to them, also their love-affairs, and the entirely relaxed nature of their daily life. Wherefore they have the character of the Hypodorian harmony, as it is called. This, Heracleides says, is in fact the one which they called Aeolian, as Lasus of Hermione does in the "Hymn to Demeter of Hermion" in the following words: "I celebrate Demeter and Kore, wedded wife of Pluto, raising unto them a sweet-voiced hymn in the deep-toned Aeolian harmony." These lyrics are sung by all in the Hypodorian. Since, then, the melody is Hypodorian, it naturally follows that Lasus calls the harmony Aeolian. Again, Pratinas says, I believe: "Pursue neither the intense Muse nor yet the relaxed Ionian, but ploughing rather the middle glebe play the Aeolian with your melody." And in what follows he says more plainly: "Verily the Aeolian harmony is the song that befits all the bold." [2] Formerly, then, as I have said, they called it Aeolian, but later Hypodorian, as some assert, because they thought that in the auloi it had a range below the Dorian harmony.[3] But I believe that people who observed the turgid quality and pretence of nobleness in the character of the Aeolian harmony, regarded it not as Dorian at all, but something which somehow resembled the Dorian; hence they called it Hypodorian, just as we say that what resembles white is rather (*hypo*-) white, or what is not sweet, yet nearly sweet, rather (*hypo*-) sweet: in similar fashion they called Hypodorian that which was not quite Dorian.

Next in order let us examine the Milesians' character, which the Ionians illustrate. Because of their excellent physical condition they bear themselves haughtily, they are full of irate spirit, hard to placate, fond of contention, never condescending to kindliness nor cheerfulness, displaying a lack of affection and a hardness in their character. Hence also the kind of music known as the Ionian harmony is neither bright nor cheerful, but austere and hard, having a seriousness which is not ignoble; and so their harmony is well-adapted to tragedy. But the character of the Ionians today is more voluptuous, and the character of their harmony is much altered. They say that Pythermus of Teos composed lyric scolia in this kind of harmony, and since the poet was an Ionian the harmony was called Ionian. This is the Pythermus mentioned by Ananius or Hipponax in their *Iambic Verses:* . . . And in another passage as follows: "Pythermus speaks of gold as if other things were naught." In fact Pythermus

---

[2] On the interpretation of these lines of Pratinas see D. B. Monro, *The Modes of Ancient Greek Music* (Oxford, 1894), pp. 5–6, and Professor Gulick's note in the Loeb Library edition of his translation (VI, 369). Since Dorian, Aeolian, and Ionian are the only harmonies under discussion in this paragraph, we may perhaps take 'the high-strung Muse" as referring to Dorian— or at least assume that the phrase was so understood by Heracleides or Athenaeus. But no matter how we take it and regardless of whether we understand the lines in a modal or in a tonal sense, the characterization of Aeolian as intermediate will be unintelligible unless we assume, as Professor Gulick implies, that it refers, not to pitch or structure, but to ethical quality.

[3] See Aristoxenus, *Harmonic Elements* (p. 29 above), where Aristoxenus explains that those predecessors of his who based their enumeration of the keys on the boring of the finger-holes on the auloi placed the Hypodorian key three dieses below the Dorian.

does speak of it thus: "Other things, after all, are naught compared with gold." And so, considering also this saying of his, it is to be believed that Pythermus, being from Ionia, made the style of his lyrics fit the character of the Ionians. Hence I assume that it was not the Ionian harmony in which Pythermus composed, but a curious variation of harmonic figure. So one should look with disdain on those who cannot see specific differences, but simply attend to the highness or lowness of notes, and assume a Hypermixolydian harmony and again another higher than that. Nor can I see, in fact, that the Hyperphrygian has a special character of its own. And yet some persons assert that they have discovered another new, Hypophrygian, harmony! But a harmony must have a specific character or feeling, like the Locrian; this was once employed by some who flourished in the time of Simonides and Pindar, but it fell into disrepute again.[4]

These harmonies, then, are three, as we said of them at the beginning, being as many as there are tribes of Greeks. The Phrygian and the Lydian harmonies, originating with the barbarians, came to be known to the Greeks from the Phrygians and Lydians who emigrated to Peloponnesus with Pelops. The Lydians accompanied him because Sipylus was a city of Lydia; the Phrygians came not only because they lived on the borders of Lydia but also because Tantalus ruled over them. You may see everywhere in Peloponnesus, but especially in Lacedaemon, large mounds, which they call the tombs of the Phrygians who came with Pelops. These musical harmonies, then, the Greeks learned from them. Hence also Telestes of Selinus says: "The first to sing the Phrygian nome in honor of the Mountain Mother, amid the auloi beside the mixing-bowls of the Greeks, were they who came in the company of Pelops; and the Greeks struck up the Lydian hymn with the high-pitched twanging of the pectis."

Polybius of Megalopolis says:[5] "One must not accept it as fact that music was introduced among men for purposes of deceit and quackery, as Ephorus asserts that it was; nor should one believe that the ancient Cretans and Lacedaemonians introduced the aulos and a marching rhythm into battle, instead of the trumpet, without good reason; nor was it by chance that the earliest Arcadians carried the art of music into their entire social organization, so that they made it obligatory and habitual not only for boys but also for young men up to thirty years of age, although in all other respects they were most austere in their habits of life. It is only

---

[4] This polemic against those who presume to add to the established harmonies is well discussed by Winnington-Ingram (*Mode in Ancient Greek Music*, Cambridge, 1936, pp. 20-21).

[5] *Histories* IV, xx, 5-21.

among the Arcadians, at any rate, that the boys, from infancy up, are by law practised in singing hymns and paeans, in which, according to ancestral custom, they celebrate their national heroes and gods. After these they learn the nomes of Timotheus and Philoxenus and dance them annually in the theatres with Dionysiac aulos-players, the boys competing in the boys' contests, the young men in the contests of adult males. And throughout their whole lives, in their social gatherings they do not pursue methods and practices so much with the aid of imported entertainments as with their own talents, requiring one another to sing each in his turn. As for other branches of training, it is no disgrace to confess that one knows nothing, but it is deemed a disgrace among them to decline to sing. What is more, they practise marching-songs with aulos accompaniment in regular order, and further, they drill themselves in dances and display them annually in the theatres with elaborate care and at public expense. All this, therefore, the men of old taught them, not to gratify luxury and wealth, but because they observed the hardness in every one's life and the austerity of their character, which are the natural accompaniment of the coldness of their environment and the gloominess prevailing for the most part in their abodes; for all of us human beings naturally become assimilated to the character of our abode; hence it is also differences in our national position that cause us to differ very greatly from one another in character, in build, and in complexion. In addition to the training just described, their ancestors taught the Arcadian men and women the practice of public assembly and sacrifice, also at the same time choruses of girls and boys, eager as they were to civilize and soften the toughness of their natures by customs regularly organized. But the people of Cynaetha came at the end to neglect these customs, although they occupied by far the rudest part of Arcadia in point of topography as well as climate; when they plunged right into friction and rivalry with one another they finally became so brutalized that among them alone occurred the gravest acts of sacrilege. At the time when they brought upon themselves the great massacre, into whatever Arcadian cities they went on their way through, all the others immediately barred them out by public proclamation, but the Mantinaeans, after their withdrawal, instituted a purification of their city, carrying the blood of slain animals round about their entire territory."

Agias, the writer on music, has said that storax, which is burned as incense in the orchestras at the festival of Dionysus, produces a "Phrygian" odor to those who smell it.

In ancient times music was an incitement to bravery. At any rate the poet Alcaeus, who certainly was very musical, if any one ever was, places deeds of bravery higher than the achievements of poetry, since he was more than ordinarily warlike. Wherefore, pluming himself on these activities, he says: "The great hall glistens with bronze; the whole roof is adorned by the War-god with shining helmets, and over them wave white plumes of horsehair, adornments for the heads of heroes; shining greaves of bronze, defence against the cruel missiles, hide the pegs on which they hang; corslets of new linen and hollow shields lie scattered on the ground, and beside them are Chalcidian swords, beside them, too, many sashes and tunics. These we must not forget, now that before all else we have set ourselves to this task." And yet it doubtless would have been more fitting for his house to be full of musical instruments. However, the men of old assumed that bravery is the highest of civic virtues, and to this they thought it right to allot most honors . . . not to other men. Archilochus, at any rate, who was an excellent poet, made it his first boast that he was able to take part in these civic rivalries, and only secondarily mentioned his poetic talents, saying: "I am the squire of the lord Enyalius, and I am versed, too, in the lovely gift of the Muses." Similarly Aeschylus also, for all the great repute which he enjoys because of his poetry, none the less thought it right to have his bravery recorded by preference on his tomb, having composed this inscription: "Of his glorious might the grove at Marathon could tell, and the long-haired Medes— for they know!"

Hence it is that the brave Lacedaemonians march to battle with the music of the auloi, the Cretans with the lyre, the Lydians with syrinxes and the auloi, as Herodotus records.[6] Many of the barbarians also conduct diplomatic negotiations to the accompaniment of the auloi and cithara to soften the hearts of their opponents. Theopompus, in the forty-sixth book of his *Histories*, says: "The Getae conduct negotiations holding citharas in their hands and playing on them." Whence it is plain that Homer observes the ancient Greek system when he says: "(We have satisfied our souls with the equal feast) and with the phorminx, which the gods have made the companion of the feast,"[7] evidently because the art is beneficial also to those who feast. And this was the accepted custom, it is plain, first in order that every one who felt impelled to get drunk and stuff himself might have music to cure his violence and intemperance, and secondly, because music appeases surliness; for, by stripping off a man's gloominess, it produces good-temper and gladness becoming to a gentleman, wherefore Homer introduced the gods, in the first part of the *Iliad*, making

---

6 *Histories,* I, 17.   7 *Odyssey,* VIII, 99; XVII, 270–271.

use of music. For after their quarrel over Achilles, they spent the time continually listening "to the beautiful phorminx that Apollo held, and to the Muses who sang responsively with beautiful voice." [8] For that was bound to stop their bickerings and faction, as we were saying. It is plain, therefore, that while most persons devote this art to social gatherings for the sake of correcting conduct and of general usefulness, the ancients went further and included in their customs and laws the singing of praises to the gods by all who attended feasts, in order that our dignity and sobriety might be retained through their help. For, since the songs are sung in concert, if discourse on the gods has been added it dignifies the mood of every one. Philochorus says that the ancients, in pouring libations, do not always sing dithyrambs, but when they pour libations, they celebrate Dionysus with wine and drunkenness, but Apollo, in quiet and good order. Archilochus, at any rate, says: "For I know how to lead off, in the lovely song of lord Dionysus, the dithyramb, when my wits have been stricken with the thunder-bolt of wine." And Epicharmus, also, said in *Philoctetes:* "There can be no dithyramb when you drink water." It is plain, therefore, in the light of what we have said, that music did not, at the beginning, make its way into feasts merely for the sake of shallow and ordinary pleasure, as some persons think. As for the Lacedaemonians, if they studied the art of music, they say nothing of it, but that they are able to judge the art well is admitted by them, and in fact they assert that they have saved the art three times when it was threatened with debasement.[9]

.   .   .   .   .

In olden times the feeling for nobility was always maintained in the art of music, and all its elements skillfully retained the orderly beauty appropriate to them. Hence there were auloi peculiarly adapted to every harmony, and every player had auloi suited to every harmony used in the public contests. But Pronomus of Thebes began the practice of playing all the harmonies on the same auloi. Today, however, people take up music in a haphazard and irrational manner. In early times popularity with the masses was a sign of bad art; hence, when a certain aulos-player once received loud applause, Asopodorus of Phlius, who was himself still waiting in the wings, said "What's this? Something awful must have happened!" The player evidently could not have won approval with the crowd otherwise. (I am aware that some persons have narrated this story with Antigeneidas as the speaker.) And yet the musicians

---

of our day set as the goal of their art success with their audiences. Hence Aristoxenus in his *Drinking-Miscellany* says: "We act like the people of Poseidonia, who dwell on the Tyrrhenian Gulf. It so happened that although they were originally Greeks, they were completely barbarized, becoming Tuscans or Romans; they changed their speech and their other practices, but they still celebrate one festival that is Greek to this day, wherein they gather together and recall those ancient words and institutions, and after bewailing them and weeping over them in one another's presence they depart home. In like manner we also (says Aristoxenus), now that our theatres have become utterly barbarized and this prostituted music has moved on into a state of grave corruption, will get together by ourselves, few though we be, and recall what the art of music used to be." So much for what Aristoxenus says.

In view of this it is plain to me also that music should be the subject of philosophic reflection. Pythagoras of Samos, with all his great fame as a philosopher, is one of many conspicuous for having taken up music as no mere hobby; on the contrary, he explains the very being of the universe as bound together by musical principles. Taking it all together, it is plain that the ancient "wisdom" of the Greeks was given over especially to music. For this reason they regarded Apollo, among the gods, and Orpheus, among the demigods, as most musical and most wise; and they called all who followed this art sophists, as Aeschylus has done: "Then the sophist wildly struck his tortoise-shell lyre with notes discordant." And that the men of old were disposed to treat music with the greatest familiarity is clear also from Homer; why, in setting all his poetry to music he often, without thought, composes verses which are "acephalous," or "slack," or even "taper off at the end." But Xenophanes, Solon, Theognis, Phocylides, also the Corinthian elegiac poet Periander and other poets who do not add melodies to their poetry, finish off their verses in respect of the counting and the arrangement of the metrical feet, and see to it that not one of them is either acephalous or slack or tapering. Acephalous verses are those which have the quality of lameness at the beginning: "When they had come to the ships and to the Hellespont." "A strap lay stretched upon it, made of a slaughtered ox's hide." Slack verses are lame in the middle, as for example: "Then quickly Aeneas, dear son of Anchises." "Their leaders, again, were the two sons of Asclepius." Tapering verses limp at the close: "The Trojans shivered when they saw the wriggling snake." "Fair Cassiepeia, like unto the gods in form." "With this wine I filled a mighty goat-skin and carried it, with provisions as well."

Of all the Greeks the Spartans have most faithfully preserved the art of music, employing it most extensively, and many composers of lyrics have arisen among them. Even to this day they carefully retain the ancient songs, and are very well taught in them and strict in holding to them. Hence Pratinas says: "The Spartan, that cicada ready for a chorus." Wherefore, also, their poets continually addressed songs in terms like these: "Leader of sweetest hymns," and "Mellifluous melodies of the Muses." For people were glad to turn from the soberness and austerity of life to the solace of music, because the art has the power to charm. With good reason, therefore, the listeners enjoyed it.

Demetrius of Byzantium, in the fourth book of his work *On Poetry*, says that they used to employ the term *choregi*, not, as today, of the men who hired the choruses, but of those who led the chorus, as the etymology of the word denotes.

Also, it was customary to practise good music and not violate the ancient rules of the art.

It happened that in ancient times the Greeks were music-lovers; but later, with the breakdown of order, when practically all the ancient customs fell into decay, this devotion to principle ceased, and debased fashions in music came to light, wherein every one who practised them substituted effeminacy for gentleness, and license and looseness for moderation. What is more, this fashion will doubtless be carried further if some one does not bring the music of our forebears once more to open practice. For in ancient times it was the acts of heroes and the praise of the gods that the poets put to song-music. Homer, for example, says of Achilles: "And he was singing the glorious deeds of men," [10] that is, of heroes. And of Phemius he says: "He knoweth many charms for mortals, deeds of men and of gods, which minstrels celebrate." [11] This custom was kept up also among the barbarians, as Dinon declares in his *Persian History*. It was the singers, for example, that foresaw the courage of the first Cyrus and the war he was to wage against Astyages. "It was at the time (says Dinon) when Cyrus requested permission to visit Persia (he had previously been in charge of Astyages' rod-bearers, and later of his men-at-arms) and had departed; Astyages, therefore, celebrated a feast in company with his friends, and on that occasion a man named Angares (he was the most distinguished of the singers) was invited, and not only began to sing other customary songs but also, at the last, he told how that a mighty beast had been let loose in the swamp, bolder than a wild boar; which beast, if it got the mastery of the regions round it, would soon contend against a multitude without difficulty. And when Astyages

---

[10] *Iliad*, IX, 189   [11] *Odyssey*, I, 337

asked, 'What beast?' he replied, 'Cyrus the Persian.' Believing, therefore, that his suspicion about him had been correct, he kept summoning him to return . . . it did no good."

Though I might say many things more on the subject of music, I hear the buzzing of the auloi, and will therefore bring my long-winded discourse to a close, after repeating the lines from *The Aulos-Lover* of Philetaerus: "Zeus, it's indeed a fine thing to die to the music of the auloi. For only to such is it permitted in Hades to revel in love affairs, whereas those whose manners are sordid, having no knowledge of music, must carry water to the leaky jar."

II

The Early Christian View of Music

6. Clement of Alexandria

Titus Flavius Clemens Alexandrinus, a Greek ecclesiastical scholar and teacher of unknown origin, lived in the second half of the second century A.D. and died before 216. Clement was originally a pagan but was later converted to the Christian faith. He undertook extensive trips and became a pupil of Pantaenus in the catechetical school of Alexandria. After his master's death he became Pantaenus' successor. Among his pupils were Origen and Alexander, bishop of Jerusalem.

In his writings, Clement shows equal familiarity with Greek epic, lyric, tragic, and comic poetry on one hand, and with Greek prose writers and philosophers on the other. His thought is a combination of ecclesiastical tradition with elements of Hellenistic philosophy. Clement regarded Christianity as a teaching that surpassed the pagan Greek philosophy in that it revealed in Christ the absolute and perfect truth. Of his works, *The Exhortation to the Greeks* is in the main a polemic against the crudities of pagan mythological stories.

From the Exhortation to the Greeks [1]

I.

AMPHION of Thebes and Arion of Methymna were both minstrels. Both are celebrated in legend, and to this day the story is sung by a chorus of Greeks how their musical skill enabled the one to lure a fish and the other to build the walls of Thebes. There was also a Thracian wizard,[2] —so runs another Greek legend,—who used to tame wild beasts simply by his song, yes, and to transplant trees, oaks, by music. I can also tell you of another legend and another minstrel akin to these, namely, Eunomus the Locrian and the Pythian grasshopper. A solemn assembly of Greeks,

1 Text: *Clement of Alexandria* (London, W. W. Heinemann, 1919), 3–17. Translated for the Loeb Classical Library by Rev. G. W. Butterworth. Reprinted by permission of Harvard University Press.

2 Orpheus.

held in honour of a dead serpent, was gathering at Pytho,[3] and Eunomus sang a funeral ode for the reptile. Whether his song was a hymn in praise of the snake, or a lamentation over it, I cannot say; but there was a competition, and Eunomus was playing the cithara in the heat of the day, at the time when the grasshoppers, warmed by the sun, were singing under the leaves along the hills. They were singing, you see, not to the dead serpent of Pytho, but to the all-wise God, a spontaneous natural song, better than the measured nomes of Eunomus. A string breaks in the Locrian's hands; the grasshopper settles upon the neck of the instrument and begins to twitter there as if upon a branch: whereupon the minstrel, by adapting his music to the grasshopper's lay, supplied the place of the missing string. So it was not Eunomus that drew the grasshopper by his song, as the legend would have it, when it set up the bronze figure at Pytho, showing Eunomus with his cithara, and his ally in the contest. No, the grasshopper flew of its own accord, and sang of its own accord, although the Greeks thought it to have been responsive to music.

How in the world is it that you have given credence to worthless legends, imagining brute beasts to be enchanted by music, while the bright face of truth seems alone to strike you as deceptive, and is regarded with unbelieving eyes? Cithaeron, and Helicon, and the mountains of Odrysians and Thracians, temples of initiation into error, are held sacred on account of the attendant mysteries, and are celebrated in hymns. For my own part, mere legend though they are, I cannot bear the thought of all the calamities that are worked up into tragedy; yet in your hands the records of these evils have become dramas, and the actors of the dramas are a sight that gladdens your heart. But as for the dramas and the Lenaean poets, who are altogether like drunken men, let us wreathe them, if you like, with ivy, while they are performing the mad revels of the Bacchic rite, and shut them up, satyrs and frenzied rout and all,—yes, and the rest of the company of daemons too,—in Helicon and Cithaeron now grown old; and let us bring down truth, with wisdom in all her brightness, from heaven above, to the holy mountain of God and the holy company of the prophets. Let truth, sending forth her rays of light into the farthest distance, shine everywhere upon those who are wallowing in darkness, and deliver men from their error, stretching out her supreme right hand, even understanding, to point them to salvation. And when they have raised their heads and looked up let them forsake Helicon and Cithaeron to dwell in Sion; "for out of Sion shall go forth the law, and the Word

---

3 Delphi. According to the Greek legend the serpent was the ancient guardian of the Delphic shrine and was slain by Apollo. [Butterworth]

of the Lord from Jerusalem," [4] that is, the heavenly Word, the true champion, who is being crowned upon the stage of the whole world. Aye, and this Eunomus of mine sings not the nome of Terpander or of Capio, nor yet in Phrygian or Lydian or Dorian; but the new harmony, with its eternal nome that bears the name of God. This is the new song, the song of Moses,

> Soother of grief and wrath, that bids all ills be forgotten. [5]

There is a sweet and genuine medicine of persuasion blended with this song.

In my opinion, therefore, our Thracian, Orpheus, and the Theban and the Methymnian too, are not worthy of the name of man, since they were deceivers. Under cover of music they have outraged human life, being influenced by daemons, through some artful sorcery, to compass man's ruin. By commemorating deeds of violence in their religious rites, and by bringing stories of sorrow into worship, they were the first to lead men by the hand to idolatry; yes, and with stocks and stones, that is to say, statues and pictures, to build up the stupidity of custom. By their chants and enchantments they have held captive in the lowest slavery that truly noble freedom which belongs to those who are citizens under heaven.

But far different is my minstrel, for He has come to bring to a speedy end the bitter slavery of the daemons that lord it over us; and by leading us back to the mild and kindly yoke of piety He calls once again to heaven those who have been cast down to earth. He at least is the only one who ever tamed the most intractable of all wild beasts—man: for he tamed birds, that is, flighty men; reptiles, that is, crafty men; lions, that is, passionate men; swine, that is, pleasure-loving men; wolves, that is, rapacious men. Men without understanding are stocks and stones; indeed a man steeped in ignorance is even more senseless than stones. As our witness let the prophetic voice, which shares in the song of truth, come forward, speaking words of pity for those who waste away their lives in ignorance and folly,—"for God is able of these stones to raise up children unto Abraham." [6] And God, in compassion for the great dullness and the hardness of those whose hearts are petrified against the truth, did raise up out of those stones, that is, the Gentiles who trust in stones, a seed of piety sensitive to virtue. Again, in one place the words "offspring of vipers" [7] are applied to certain venomous and deceitful hypocrites, who lie in wait against righteousness; yet if any even of these snakes chooses to repent,

---

4 Isaiah 2:3.
5 Homer, *Odyssey*, iv, 221.
6 Matthew 3:9; Luke 3:8.
7 Matthew 3:7; Luke 3:7.

let him but follow the Word and he becomes a "man of God." [8] Others are figuratively called "wolves" [9] clothed in sheepskins, by which is meant rapacious creatures in the forms of men. And all these most savage beasts, and all such stones, the heavenly song of itself transformed into men of gentleness. "For we, yea we also were aforetime foolish, disobedient, deceived, serving divers lusts and pleasures, living in malice and envy, hateful, hating one another," as the apostolic writing says; "but when the kindness of God our Saviour, and His love toward man, appeared, not by works done in righteousness, which we did ourselves, but according to His mercy He saved us." [10]

See how mighty is the new song! It has made men out of stones and men out of wild beasts. They who were otherwise dead, who had no share in the real and true life, revived when they but heard the song. Furthermore, it is this which composed the entire creation into melodious order, and tuned into concert the discord of the elements, that the whole universe might be in harmony with it.[11] The ocean it left flowing, yet has prevented it from encroaching upon the land; whereas the land, which was being carried away, it made firm, and fixed as a boundary to the sea. Aye, and it softened the rage of fire by air, as one might blend the Dorian harmony with the Lydian; and the biting coldness of air it tempered by the intermixture of fire, thus melodiously mingling these extreme notes of the universe. What is more, this pure song, the stay of the universe and the harmony of all things, stretching from the centre to the circumference and from the extremities to the centre, reduced this whole to harmony, not in accordance with Thracian music,[12] which resembles that of Jubal, but in accordance with the fatherly purpose of God, which David earnestly sought. He who sprang from David and yet was before him, the Word of God, scorned those lifeless instruments of lyre and cithara. By the power of the Holy Spirit He arranged in harmonious order this great world, yes, and the little world of man too, body and soul together; and on this many-voiced instrument of the universe He makes music to God, and sings to the human instrument. "For thou art my harp and my pipe and my temple" [13]—my harp by reason of the music, my pipe by reason of the breath of the Spirit, my temple by reason of the Word—God's purpose being that the music should resound, the Spirit inspire, and the temple

8 I Timothy 6:11.

9 Matthew 7:15.

10 Titus 3:3–5.

11 Having credited to the New Song the wonders attributed by Greek legend to Orpheus, Amphion, and Arion, Clement now goes on to identify with it the harmonic principle, in accordance with which the Pythagoreans held the cosmos and the human microcosmos to have been formed from the four elements—water, earth, fire, and air.

12 The music of Orpheus.

13 The source of this quotation is unknown. It may be a fragment of an early Christian hymn, the metaphors being suggested by such passages as Psalm 57:8; I Corinthians 6:19. [Butterworth]

receive its Lord. Moreover, King David the harpist, whom we mentioned just above, urged us toward the truth and away from idols. So far was he from singing the praises of daemons that they were put to flight by him with the true music; and when Saul was possessed, David healed him merely by playing the harp.[14] The Lord fashioned man a beautiful, breathing instrument, after His own image; and assuredly He Himself is an all-harmonious instrument of God, melodious and holy, the wisdom that is above this world, the heavenly Word.

What then is the purpose of this instrument, the Word of God, the Lord, and the New Song? To open the eyes of the blind, to unstop the ears of the deaf, and to lead the halt and erring into the way of righteousness; to reveal God to foolish men, to make an end of corruption, to vanquish death, to reconcile disobedient sons to the Father. The instrument of God is loving to men. The Lord pities, chastens, exhorts, admonishes, saves, and guards us; and, over and above this, promises the kingdom of heaven as reward for our discipleship, while the only joy He has of us is that we are saved. For wickedness feeds upon the corruption of men; but truth, like the bee, does no harm to anything in the world, but takes delight only in the salvation of men. You have then God's promise; you have His love to man: partake of His grace.

And do not suppose that my song of salvation is new in the same sense as an implement or a house. For it was "before the morning star"; [15] and, "in the beginning was the Word, and the Word was with God, and the Word was God." [16] But error is old, and truth appears to be a new thing. Whether then the Phrygians are really proved to be ancient by the goats in the story; [17] or the Arcadians by the poets who describe them as older than the moon; or, again, the Egyptians by those who dream that this land first brought to light both gods and men; still, not one of these nations existed before this world. But we were before the foundation of the world, we who, because we were destined to be in Him, were begotten beforehand by God. We are the rational images formed by God's Word, or Reason, and we date from the beginning on account of our connection with Him, because "the Word was in the beginning." Well, because the Word was from the first, He was and is the divine beginning of all things; but because He lately took a name,—the name consecrated of old and worthy of power, the Christ,—I have called Him a New Song.

14 I Samuel 16:23.
15 Psalm 110:3.
16 John 1:1.
17 See the story in Herodotus, ii, 2. Psammetichus, king of Egypt, being desirous of discovering which was the most ancient people, put two children in charge of a herdsman. Goats were to be brought to them for giving milk, but no articulate speech was to be uttered in their presence. The first articulate sound they made was taken to be the Phrygian word for bread; hence the king assumed that Phrygians were the primitive race. [Butterworth]

7. St. Basil

St. Basil was born at Caesarea, Cappadocia, about 330 A.D. Surnamed The Great, he studied at Constantinople and Athens, was baptized in 357, and after extensive travels retired to the desert of Pontus and there founded a monastic order called the Basilians. He became bishop of Caesarea in 370 and died in 378.

St. Basil was important as a preacher (*Homilies*) and a theologian, and earned a prominent name in the early life of the Church by his efforts to settle the Arian dispute and to develop monastic institutions. The liturgy of St. Basil is still used in the Eastern Church.

From the Homily on the First Psalm [1]

1. ALL SCRIPTURE is given by inspiration of God and is profitable [2] and was composed by the Holy Spirit to the end that, as in a common dispensary for souls, we may, all men, select each the medicine for his own disease. For the Scripture saith, "Medicine pacifieth great offenses." [3] The Prophets therefore teach certain things, the Histories others, the Law others, and the kind of counsel given in the Proverbs others. But the book of the Psalms embraces whatever in all the others is helpful. It prophesies things to come, it recalls histories to the mind, it gives laws for living, it counsels what is to be done. And altogether it is a storehouse of good instructions, diligently providing for each what is useful to him. For it heals the ancient wounds of souls and to the newly wounded brings prompt relief; it ministers to what is sick and preserves what is in health; and it wholly removes the ills, howsoever great and of whatsoever kind, that attack souls in our human life; and this by means of a certain well-timed persuasion which inspires wholesome reflection.

1 Text: Migne, *Patrologia graeca*, XXIX, 209-213. 2 II Timothy 3:16. 8 Ecclesiastes 10:4.

For when the Holy Spirit saw that mankind was ill-inclined toward virtue and that we were heedless of the righteous life because of our inclination to pleasure, what did He do? He blended the delight of melody with doctrines in order that through the pleasantness and softness of the sound we might unawares receive what was useful in the words, according to the practice of wise physicians, who, when they give the more bitter draughts to the sick, often smear the rim of the cup with honey. For this purpose these harmonious melodies of the Psalms have been designed for us, that those who are of boyish age or wholly youthful in their character, while in appearance they sing, may in reality be educating their souls. For hardly a single one of the many, and even of the indolent, has gone away retaining in his memory any precept of the apostles or of the prophets, but the oracles of the Psalms they both sing at home and disseminate in the market place. And if somewhere one who rages like a wild beast from excessive anger falls under the spell of the psalm, he straightway departs, with the fierceness of his soul calmed by the melody.

2. A psalm is the tranquillity of souls, the arbitrator of peace, restraining the disorder and turbulence of thoughts, for it softens the passion of the soul and moderates its unruliness. A psalm forms friendships, unites the divided, mediates between enemies. For who can still consider him an enemy with whom he has sent forth one voice to God? So that the singing of psalms brings love, the greatest of good things, contriving harmony like some bond of union and uniting the people in the symphony of a single choir.

A psalm drives away demons, summons the help of angels, furnishes arms against nightly terrors, and gives respite from daily toil; to little children it is safety, to men in their prime an adornment, to the old a solace, to women their most fitting ornament. It peoples solitudes, it chastens market places. To beginners it is a beginning; to those who are advancing, an increase; to those who are concluding, a support. A psalm is the voice of the church. It gladdens feast days, it creates the grief which is in accord with God's will, for a psalm brings a tear even from a heart of stone.

A psalm is the work of the angels, the ordinance of Heaven, the incense of the Spirit. Oh, the wise invention of the teacher who devised how we might at the same time sing and learn profitable things, whereby doctrines are somehow more deeply impressed upon the mind!

What is learned unwillingly does not naturally remain, but things which are received with pleasure and love fix themselves more firmly in our minds. For what can we not learn from the Psalms? Can we not learn the splendor of courage, the exactness of justice, the dignity of self-control, the habit of repentance, the measure of patience, whatsoever good things that you may name? Here is perfect theology; here is foretold the incarnation of Christ; here are the threat of judgment, the hope of resurrection, the fear of punishment, the assurances of glory, the revelations of mysteries; all things are brought together in the book of Psalms as in some great and common storehouse.

Although there are many musical instruments, the prophet made this book suited to the psaltery, as it is called, revealing, it seems to me, the grace from on high which sounded in him through the Holy Spirit, since this alone, of all musical instruments, has the source of its sound above. For the brass wires of the cithara and the lyre sound from below against the plectrum, but the psaltery has the origins of its harmonious rhythms above, in order that we may study to seek for those things which are on high and not be drawn down by the pleasantness of the melody to the passions of the flesh.[4] And I think that by reason of this structure of the instrument the words of the prophet profoundly and wisely reveal to us that those whose souls are attuned and harmonious have an easy path to things above. But now let us examine the beginning of the Psalms.

·   ·   ·   ·   ·

---

[4] For this comparison and the various symbolic interpretations placed on it by the Church Fathers see Hermann Abert, *Die Musikanschauung des Mittelalters* (Halle, 1905), pp. 215–218, and Théodore Gérold, *Les Pères de l'église et la musique* (Paris, 1931), pp. 126–130.

8. St. John Chrysostom

St. John was born in Antioch about 345 A.D. He studied with the rhetorician Libanius, was ordained a priest, and in 397 became Bishop of Constantinople. A famous Greek Father, patron of preachers, he was surnamed *Chrysostomos* ("the golden-mouthed") on account of his impressive oratorical skill. Because of his zealous efforts to improve the moral standing of laymen and clerics alike, Chrysostom was twice deposed and sent into exile. The second time, in 404, he was banished first to Armenia, later to Pontus, and died in exile in 407.

St. John Chrysostom was one of the most important preachers of early Christianity. In his writings, he was more concerned with the practical and moral aspects of theology than with its theoretical and dogmatic aspects. This fact accounts for his being considered the greatest moralist among the ancient Christian theologians.

From the Exposition of Psalm XLI [1]

WHEN GOD saw that many men were rather indolent, that they came unwillingly to Scriptural readings and did not endure the labor this involves, wishing to make the labor more grateful and to take away the sensation of it, He blended melody with prophecy in order that, delighted by the modulation of the chant, all might with great eagerness give forth sacred hymns to Him. For nothing so uplifts the mind, giving it wings and freeing it from the earth, releasing it from the chains of the body, affecting it with love of wisdom, and causing it to scorn all things pertaining to this life, as modulated melody and the divine chant composed of number.

To such an extent, indeed, is our nature delighted by chants and songs that even infants at the breast, if they be weeping or afflicted, are by reason of it lulled to sleep. Nurses, carrying them in their arms, walking to and

1 Text: Migne, *Patrologia graeca*, LV, 155–159.

fro and singing certain childish songs to them, often cause them to close their eyes. For this reason travelers also, driving at noon the yoked animals, sing as they do so, lightening by their chants the hardships of the journey. And not only travelers, but also peasants often sing as they tread the grapes in the wine press, gather the vintage, tend the vine, and perform their other tasks. Sailors do likewise, pulling at the oars. Women, too, weaving and parting the tangled threads with the shuttle, often sing a certain single melody, sometimes individually and to themselves, sometimes all together in concert. This they do, the women, travelers, peasants, and sailors, striving to lighten with a chant the labor endured in working, for the mind suffers hardships and difficulties more easily when it hears songs and chants.

Inasmuch as this kind of pleasure is thoroughly innate to our mind, and lest demons introducing lascivious songs should overthrow everything, God established the psalms, in order that singing might be both a pleasure and a help. From strange chants harm, ruin, and many grievous matters are brought in, for those things that are lascivious and vicious in all songs settle in parts of the mind, making it softer and weaker; from the spiritual psalms, however, proceeds much of value, much utility, much sanctity, and every inducement to philosophy, for the words purify the mind and the Holy Spirit descends swiftly upon the mind of the singer. For those who sing with understanding invoke the grace of the Spirit.

Hear what Paul says: "Be not drunk with wine, wherein is excess, but be filled with the Spirit." He adds, moreover, what the cause of this filling is: "Singing and making melody in your heart to the Lord." [2] What is the meaning of "in your heart"? With understanding, he says; not so that the mouth utters words while the mind is inattentive, wandering in all directions, but so that the mind may hear the tongue.

And as swine flock together where there is a mire, but where there is aroma and incense there bees abide, so demons congregate where there are licentious chants, but where there are spiritual ones there the grace of the Spirit descends, sanctifying mouth and mind. This I say, not only that you may yourselves sing praises, but also that you may teach your wives and children to do so, not merely while weaving, to lighten the work, but especially at the table. For since Satan, seeking to ensnare us at feasts, for the most part employs as allies drunkenness, gluttony, immoderate laughter, and an inactive mind; at this time, both before and after table, it is especially necessary to fortify oneself with the protection

---

[2] Ephesians 5:18, 19.

of the psalms and, rising from the feast together with one's wife and children, to sing sacred hymns to God.

For if Paul, imprisoned, made fast in the stocks, and threatened with intolerable scourges, with Silas praised God continually at midnight, when sleep is most pleasant to everyone, and neither the place, nor the hour, nor his anxieties, nor the tyrant's slumbers, nor the pain of his labors, nor anything else could bring him to interrupt his singing,[3] so much the more ought we, who live pleasantly and enjoy God's blessings, to give forth hymns expressing thanks to Him.

What if drunkenness or gluttony does make our minds dull and foolish? Where psalmody has entered, all these evil and depraved counsels retreat.

And just as not a few wealthy persons wipe off their tables with a sponge filled with balsam, so that if any stain remain from the food, they may remove it and show a clean table; so should we also, filling our mouths with spiritual melody instead of balsam, so that if any stain remain in our mind from the abundance, we may thereby wipe it away.

And all standing, let us say together: "For thou, Lord, hast made me glad through thy work; I will triumph in the works of thy hands." [4] Then after the psalmody let there be added a prayer, in order that along with the mind we may also make holy the house itself.

And as those who bring comedians, dancers, and harlots into their feasts call in demons and Satan himself and fill their homes with innumerable contentions (among them jealousy, adultery, debauchery, and countless evils); so those who invoke David with his lyre call inwardly on Christ. Where Christ is, let no demon enter; let him not even dare to look in in passing. Peace, delight, and all good things flow here as from fountains. Those make their home a theatre; make yours a church. For where there are psalms, and prayers, and the dance of the prophets, and singers with pious intentions, no one will err if he call the assembly a church.

Even though the meaning of the words be unknown to you, teach your mouth to utter them meanwhile. For the tongue is made holy by the words when they are uttered with a ready and eager mind. Once we have acquired this habit, neither through free will nor through carelessness shall we neglect our beautiful office; custom compelling us, even against our will, to carry out this worship daily. Nor will anyone, in such singing, be blamed if he be weakened by old age, or young, or have a harsh voice, or no knowledge at all of numbers. What is here sought for is a sober mind, an awakened intelligence, a contrite heart, sound reason, and clear

---

3 Acts 16:25.   4 Psalms 92:4.

conscience. If having these you have entered into God's sacred choir, you may stand beside David himself.

Here there is no need for the cithara, or for stretched strings, or for the plectrum, or for art, or for any instrument; but, if you like, you may yourself become a cithara, mortifying the members of the flesh and making a full harmony of mind and body.[5] For when the flesh no longer lusts against the Spirit,[6] but has submitted to its orders and has been led at length into the best and most admirable path, then will you create a spiritual melody.

Here there is no need for art which is slowly perfected; there is need only for lofty purpose, and we become skilled in a brief decisive moment. Here there is no need for place or for season; in all places and at all seasons you may sing with the mind. For whether you walk in the market place, or begin a journey, or sit down with your friends you may rouse up your mind or call out silently. So also Moses called out, and God heard him.[7] If you are an artisan, you may sing sitting and working in your shop. If you are a soldier, or if you sit in judgment, you may do the very same. One may also sing without voice, the mind resounding inwardly. For we sing, not to men, but to God, who can hear our hearts and enter into the silences of our minds.

In proof of this, Paul also cries out: "Likewise the Spirit also helpeth our infirmities. And he that searcheth the hearts knoweth what is the mind of the Spirit, because he maketh intercession for the saints according to the will of God." [8] This does not mean that the Spirit groans; it means that spiritual men, having the gifts of the Spirit, praying for their kinsmen and offering supplications, do so with contrition and groanings. Let us also do this, daily conversing with God in psalms and prayers. And let us not offer mere words, but let us know the very meaning of our speeches.

---

[5] For further examples of this figurative treatment of musical instruments, see Hermann Abert, *Die Musikanschauung des Mittelalters* (Halle, 1905), pp. 211–223.

[6] Galatians 5:17.
[7] Exodus 14:15.
[8] Romans 8:26, 27.

9. St. Jerome

Eusebius Sophronius Hieronymus, Christian saint, Church Father, patron of the theologians, was born about 340 A.D. at Stridon in Dalmatia. He studied Latin literature and Greek philosophy under Donatus and other masters in Rome. Baptized in 360, Jerome returned to Stridon an accomplished scholar. He then started on extensive travels, first to Gaul, then to the East, in the course of which he resolved henceforth to devote his scholarship to the Holy Scriptures. In 379 he was ordained a presbyter in Antioch and went to Constantinople to perfect himself in Greek. In 382, he was called to Rome, where Pope Damasus suggested to him to revise the old Latin translation of the Bible. The result of Jerome's protracted labor was the Latin translation of the Scriptures, which later became known under the name of the Vulgate or Authorized Version. Most of this work was done in Palestine, where Jerome had retired after Pope Damasus' death in 384, and where he died in September 420.

St. Jerome is "the great Christian scholar of his age rather than the profound theologian." Besides being the author of the Vulgate with which his name is forever coupled, St. Jerome left other important works in various fields of knowledge. His *Commentaries* are valuable because of his knowledge of Greek and Hebrew, and he is considered a pioneer in the fields of patrology and of biblical archeology. His *De viris illustribus* is a kind of ecclesiastical literary history.

From the Commentary on the Epistle of Paul to the Ephesians [1]

"SPEAKING to yourselves in psalms and hymns and spiritual songs, singing and making melody in your heart to the Lord." [2]

He who has kept himself from the drunkenness of wine, wherein is

---

[1] Text: Migne, *Patrologia latina*, XXVI, 561–562.　　[2] Ephesians 5:19.

excess, and has thereby been filled with the Spirit, is able to accept all things spiritually—psalms, hymns, and songs. How the psalm, the hymn, and the song differ from one another we learn most fully in the Psalter. Here let us say briefly that hymns declare the power and majesty of the Lord and continually praise his works and favors, something which all those psalms contain to which the word "Alleluia" is prefixed or appended. Psalms, moreover, properly affect the seat of the *ethos* in order that by means of this organ of the body we may know what ought to be done and what ought not to be done. The subtle moralist, however, who inquires into these things and examines the harmony of the world and the order and concord of all creatures, sings a spiritual song. To express our opinion more clearly to the simple-minded, the psalm is directed toward the body, the song toward the mind. We ought, then, to sing and to make melody and to praise the Lord more with the heart than with the voice.

This, indeed, is what is written: "Singing and making melody in your heart to the Lord." Let youth hear this, let them hear it whose office it is to make melody in the church: Sing to God, not with the voice, but with the heart; not, after the fashion of tragedians, in smearing the throat with a sweet drug, so that theatrical melodies and songs are heard in the church, but in fear, in work, and in knowledge of the Scriptures. And although a man be *kakophonos*, to use a common expression, if he have good works, he is a sweet singer before God. And let the servant of Christ sing so that he pleases, not through his voice, but through the words which he pronounces, in order that the evil spirit which was upon Saul [3] may depart from those who are similarly troubled and may not enter into those who would make of the house of God a popular theatre.

---

[3] I Samuel 16:23.

10. St. Augustine

Aurelius Augustinus, one of the most distinguished of the Church Fathers, was born at Tagaste in Numidia (North Africa) in 354 A.D. After a period of spiritual crisis in his youth, Augustine in 384 went to Milan, where he came under the influence of St. Ambrose, the bishop of that city, who converted him to the Christian faith and baptized him in 387, together with his pupil Alypius and his son Adeodatus. Augustine then returned to Africa, where his reputation had continued to grow and in 395 was made Bishop of Hippo Regius (now Bone in Algeria). There he died in 430.

St. Augustine is the author of numerous works which have exerted the most profound influence upon the development of the Catholic doctrine, indeed of all Christian doctrine. Most famous among his writings are his *Confessions,* in which Augustine gave an account of the intellectual and moral crises that led to his conversion, and the voluminous work *De civitate Dei.* St. Augustine's writings contain important references to musical practice in the early Christian Church, particularly to the so-called Ambrosian Chant. Book X of his *Confessions* deals, among other things, with problems of musical aesthetics. A tract by St. Augustine, preserved under the title *De musica,* is largely devoted to questions of meter and versification.

From the Confessions [1]

XXXIII. THE PLEASURES TAKEN IN HEARING

THE DELIGHTS of mine ears, verily, have heretofore more strongly inveigled and engaged me; but thou hast brought me off and freed me. Yet still at hearing of those airs which thy words breathe soul into, whenas they are sung with a well tuned and well governed voice, I do, I confess,

1 Text: *St. Augustine's Confessions,* II (London, W. Heinemann, 1912), 165–169. Translated by William Watts (1631) and reprinted in the Loeb Classical Library. Reprinted here by permission of Harvard University Press.

receive a little contentment; not so great though as that I am enchanted by it, but that I can go away when I please. But yet for all this, that those airs may together with these words (by virtue of which they receive life) gain full admission with me, do they aspire to be entertained into a place of no mean honor in this heart of mine, nor can I scarce afford them a room befitting for them. For sometimes forsooth, do I seem to myself to attribute more respect unto them than is seemly; yea, even whilst together with those sacred ditties I perceive our minds to be far more religiously and zealously blown up into a flame of devotion, whenas these ditties are thus sung, than they would have been, had they not been so sung: yea, and I perceive withal, how that the several affections of our spirit, have their proper moods answerable to their variety in the voice and singing, and by some secret association therewith they be stirred up. But this contentment of my flesh (unto which it is not fit to give over the mind to be enervated) doth very often beguile me: the sense going not so along with the reason, as patiently to come behind it; but having for reason's sake gained admission, it strives even to run before and be her leader. Thus in these things I sometimes sin at unawares, but afterwards am aware of it.

Again at another time, through an indiscreet weariness of being in veigled, do I err out of too precise a severity: yea, very fierce am I some times, in the desire of having the melody of all pleasant music, to which David's Psalter is so often sung, banished both from mine own ears, and out of the whole church too: and the safer way it seems unto me, which I remember to have been often told me of Athanasius Bishop of Alexan dria,[2] who caused the reader of the psalm to sound it forth with so little warbling of the voice, as that it was nearer to speaking, than to singing. Notwithstanding, so often as I call to mind the tears I shed at the hearing of thy church songs, in the beginning of my recovered faith, yea, and at this very time, whenas I am moved not with the singing, but with the thing sung (when namely they are set off with a clear voice and suitable modulation), I then acknowledge the great good use of this institution. Thus float I between peril of pleasure, and an approved profitable custom: inclined the more (though herein I pronounce no irrevocable opinion) to allow of the old usage of singing in the Church; that so by the delight taken in at the ears, the weaker minds be roused up into some feeling of devotion. And yet again, so oft as it befalls me to be more moved with the voice than with the ditty, I confess myself to have grievously offended: at which time I wish rather not to have heard the music. See now in what

2 St. Athanasius (293–373)

a state I am! Weep with me, and weep for me, O all you, who inwardly feel any thoughts, whence good actions do proceed. As for you that feel none such, these things move not you. But thou, O Lord my God, look upon me, hearken, and behold, and pity, and heal me, thou in whose eyes I am now become a problem to myself; and that is my infirmity.

III

Music as a Liberal Art

11. Boethius

A Roman statesman, philosopher, and mathematician, Boethius—in full Anicius Manlius Torquatus Severinus—was born in Rome about 480 A.D. Descended from an old and distinguished family, he became Consul in 510 and subsequently counselor to Theodoric, king of the Ostrogoths, who threw him into prison and finally executed him in 524 on charges of treason.

Boethius, together with Cassiodorus, was the chief author who through his writings transmitted the knowledge of ancient Greek music to the Middle Ages. The numerous manuscript copies of his *De institutione musica* preserved in various libraries testify to the popularity of the work during those remote centuries. It was the first printed in 1491–92 in a complete edition of Boethius' writings.

From the De institutione musica [1]

Book One

I. INTRODUCTION

MUSIC IS RELATED TO US BY NATURE AND CAN ENNOBLE OR CORRUPT THE CHARACTER

THE PERCEPTIVE power of all the senses is so spontaneously and naturally present in certain living creatures that to conceive of an animal without senses is impossible. But a scrutiny of the mind will not yield to the same degree a knowledge and clear understanding of the senses themselves. It is easily understood that we use our senses in understanding sensible things, but what in truth is the nature of the actual senses in conformity with which we act, and what is the peculiar property of sensible things,

---

1 Text: Edited by Gottfried Friedlein (Leipzig, 1867), pp. 178–189, 223–225.

is not so apparent or intelligible save by proper investigation and reflection upon the facts.

For sight is common to all mortals, but whether it results from images coming to the eye or from rays sent out to the object of sight is doubtful to the learned, though the vulgar are unaware that such doubt exists. Again, any one seeing a triangle or square easily recognizes what he sees, but to know the nature of a square or triangle he must inquire of a mathematician.

The same may be said of other matters of sense, especially of the judgment of the ear, whose power so apprehends sounds that it not only judges them and knows their differences, but is often delighted when the modes are sweet and well-ordered, and pained when disordered and incoherent ones offend the sense.

From this it follows that, of the four mathematical disciplines, the others are concerned with the pursuit of truth, but music is related not only to speculation but to morality as well. Nothing is more characteristic of human nature than to be soothed by sweet modes and stirred up by their opposites. Nor is this limited to particular professions or ages, but is common to all professions; and infants, youths, and the old as well are so naturally attuned to musical modes by a kind of spontaneous feeling that no age is without delight in sweet song. From this may be discerned the truth of what Plato not idly said, that the soul of the universe is united by musical concord.[2] For when, by means of what in ourselves is well and fitly ordered, we apprehend what in sounds is well and fitly combined, and take pleasure in it, we recognize that we ourselves are united by this likeness. For likeness is agreeable, unlikeness hateful and contrary.

From this source, also, the greatest alterations of character arise. A lascivious mind takes pleasure in the more lascivious modes, or often hearing them is softened and corrupted. Contrariwise, a sterner mind either finds joy in the more stirring modes or is aroused by them. This is why the musical modes are called by the names of peoples, as the Lydian and Phrygian modes, for whatever mode each people, as it were, delights in is named after it. For a people takes pleasure in modes resembling its own character, nor could it be that the soft should be akin to or delight the hard, or the hard delight the softer, but, as I have said, it is likeness which causes love and delight. For this reason Plato holds that any change in music of right moral tendency should be especially avoided, declaring that there could be no greater detriment to the morals of a community than a gradual perversion of chaste and modest music.[3]

2 *Timaeus*, 37A.   3 *Republic*, 424B–424C.

For the minds of those hearing it are immediately affected and gradually go astray, retaining no trace of honesty and right, if either the lascivious modes implant something shameful in their minds, or the harsher modes something savage and monstrous.

For discipline has no more open pathway to the mind than through the ear. When by this path rhythms and modes have reached the mind, it is evident that they also affect it and conform it to their nature. This may be seen in peoples. Ruder peoples delight in the harsher modes of the Thracians; civilized peoples, in more restrained modes; though in these days this almost never occurs. Since humanity is now lascivious and effeminate, it is wholly captivated by scenic and theatrical modes. Music was chaste and modest so long as it was played on simpler instruments, but since it has come to be played in a variety of manners and confusedly, it has lost the mode of gravity and virtue and fallen almost to baseness, preserving only a remnant of its ancient beauty.

This is why Plato prescribes that boys should not be trained in all modes, but only in those which are strong and simple.[4] And we should above all bear in mind that if in such a matter a series of very slight changes is made, a fresh change will not be felt, but later will create a great difference and will pass through the sense of hearing into the mind. Hence Plato considers that music of the highest moral quality and chastely composed, so that it is modest and simple and masculine, and not effeminate or savage or ill-assorted, is a great guardian of the commonwealth.[5]

This the Lacedaemonians insured when Thaletas, of Gortyna in Crete, brought to their city at great expense, was training boys in the art of music.[6] This was customary among ancient peoples and long endured. When Timotheus of Miletus added a single string to those which he found already in use and made music more complicated, he was expelled from Laconia [7] by a decree which I give in the original Greek words, premising that Spartan speech has the peculiarity of converting the letter *sigma* into *rho*:

Whereas Timotheus the Milesian, having come to our city, has dishonored the ancient music; and whereas, by discarding the seven-stringed cithara and

---

4 *Ibid.*, 399C (p. 5 above).
5 *Ibid.*, 401D (p. 8 above).
6 Cf. Plutarch, *De musica*, 1146C.
7 Athenaeus (636E) tells this story in another form: "Artemon, in the first book of his work *On the Dionysiac Guild,* says that Timotheus of Miletus is held by most authorities to have adopted an arrangement of strings with too great a number, namely the magadis; wherefore he was even about to be disciplined by the Lacedaemonians for trying to corrupt their ancient music, and some

one was on the point of cutting away his superfluous strings when he pointed to a small image of Apollo among them holding a lyre with the same number and arrangement of strings as his own, and so was acquitted" (From the translation by C. B. Gulick for the Loeb Classical Library). According to Pausanius (III, xii), the Lacedaemonians hung the cithara of Timotheus in the Scias to express their disapproval of his innovation, the addition of four new strings to the seven old ones. See also Plutarch, *De musica*, 1144F.

introducing a multiplicity of tones, he corrupts the ears of the young; and whereas, by the use of many strings and by the novelty of his melody, he decks music out as ignoble and intricate instead of simple and orderly, embellishing the melody with the chromatic genus instead of the enharmonic . . . to the antistrophic response; and whereas further, invited to take part in the contest of the Eleusinian Demeter, he suggests unseemly thoughts to the young by tricking out unbecomingly the myth of the pangs of Semele;

It is decreed concerning these matters, with Divine favor, that the Kings and Ephors shall censure Timotheus and compel him to cut away the superfluous strings of the eleven, leaving the seven, in order that everyone, heeding the dignity of the city, may beware of introducing anything ignoble into Sparta and that the good name of the contests may never be impaired.[8]

This decree sets forth that the Spartans were indignant at Timotheus the Milesian, because by complicating music he had harmed the minds of the boys whom he had taken as pupils and had turned them from the modesty of virtue, and because he had perverted harmony, which he found modest, into the chromatic genus, which is more effeminate. Such was their zeal for music that they believed it to take possession of the mind.

Indeed, it is well known how often song has overcome anger, how many wonders it has performed in affections of the body or mind. Who is unaware that Pythagoras, by means of a spondaic melody, calmed and restored to self-mastery a youth of Taormina who had become wrought up by the sound of the Phrygian mode? For when, one night, a certain harlot was in his rival's house, with the doors locked, and the youth in his frenzy was about to set fire to the house and Pythagoras was observing the motion of the stars, as his custom was; learning that the youth, wrought up by the sound of the Phrygian mode, was deaf to the many pleas of his friends to restrain him from the crime, he directed them to change the mode, and thus reduced the youth's fury to a state of perfect calm.

Cicero, in his *De consiliis,* tells the story differently, in this manner: "But if I may compare a trifling matter to a weighty one, struck by some similarity, it is said that when certain drunken youths, aroused, as is wont to happen, by the music of the tibiae, were about to break into the house of a modest woman, Pythagoras urged the player to play a spondaic melody. When he had done this, the slowness of the measures and the gravity of the player calmed their wanton fury."

To add briefly a few more illustrations, Terpander and Arion of

---

8 Perhaps the oldest forged document known to musical history. Wilamowitz, who suggests some emendations in the text (*Timotheus: Die Perser,* Leipzig, 1903, pp. 69–71), places it in the second century B.C. and calls it "a potpourri of every conceivable dialectal anomaly."

Methymna rescued the Lesbians and the Ionians from the gravest maladies by the aid of song. Then Ismenias the Theban, when the torments of sciatica were troubling a number of Boeotians, is reported to have rid them of all their afflictions by his melodies. And Empedocles, when an infuriated youth drew his sword upon a guest of his for having passed sentence upon his father, is said to have altered the mode of the singing and thus to have tempered the young man's anger.

Indeed, the power of the art of music became so evident through the studies of ancient philosophy that the Pythagoreans used to free themselves from the cares of the day by certain melodies, which caused a gentle and quiet slumber to steal upon them. Similarly, upon rising, they dispelled the stupor and confusion of sleep by certain other melodies, knowing that the whole structure of soul and body is united by musical harmony. For the impulses of the soul are stirred by emotions corresponding to the state of the body, as Democritus is said to have informed the physician Hippocrates, who came to treat him when he was in custody as a lunatic, being so regarded by all his fellow townsmen.

But to what purpose all these examples? For there can be no doubt that the state of our soul and body seems somehow to be combined together by the same proportions as our later discussion will show to combine and link together the modulations of harmony. Hence it is that sweet singing delights even children, whereas any harsh sound interrupts their pleasure in listening. Indeed, this is experienced by all ages and both sexes; though they differ in their actions, they are united by their enjoyment of music.

Why do the sorrowing, in their lamentations, express their very grief with musical modulations? This is especially a habit of women, to make the cause of their weeping seem the sweeter with some song. It was also an ancient custom that the music of the tibia preceded funeral lamentations, as witness the lines of Statius:

> The tibia with curving end,
> Wont to lead the funeral rites of tender shades,
> Sounds a deep note.[9]

And he who cannot sing agreeably still hums something to himself, not because what he sings gives him pleasure, but because one takes delight in giving outward expression to an inner pleasure, no matter what the manner.

Is it not evident that the spirit of warriors is roused by the sound of the trumpets? If it is true that a peaceful state of mind can be converted into

---

9 *Thebaid*, vi, 120–121.

wrath and fury, then beyond doubt a gentler mode can temper the wrath and passionate desire of a perturbed mind. What does it signify that when anyone's ears and mind are pleased by a melody, he involuntarily keeps time by some bodily motion and his memory garners some strain of it? From all this appears the clear and certain proof that music is so much a part of our nature that we cannot do without it even if we wish to do so.

The power of the mind should therefore be directed to the purpose of comprehending by science what is inherent by nature. Just as in the study of vision, the learned are not content to behold colors and forms without investigating their properties, so they are not content to be delighted by melodies without knowing by what proportion of sounds these are inter-related.

2. THE THREE KINDS OF MUSIC, WITH A CONSIDERATION OF THE POWER OF MUSIC

A writer upon music should therefore state at the beginning how many kinds of music those who have investigated the subject are known to have recognized. There are three kinds: the first, the music of the universe; the second, human music; the third, instrumental music, as that of the cithara or the tibiae or the other instruments which serve for melody.

The first, the music of the universe, is especially to be studied in the combining of the elements and the variety of the seasons which are observed in the heavens. How indeed could the swift mechanism of the sky move silently in its course? And although this sound does not reach our ears (as must for many reasons be the case), the extremely rapid motion of such great bodies could not be altogether without sound, especially since the courses of the stars are joined together by such mutual adaptation that nothing more equally compacted or united could be imagined. For some are borne higher and others lower, and all are revolved with a just impulse, and from their different inequalities an established order of their courses may be deduced. For this reason an established order of modulation cannot be lacking in this celestial revolution.

Now unless a certain harmony united the differences and contrary powers of the four elements, how could they form a single body and mechanism? But all this diversity produces the variety of seasons and fruits, and thereby makes the year a unity. Wherefore if you could imagine any one of the factors which produce such a variety removed, all would perish, nor, so to speak, would they retain a vestige of consonance. And just as there is a measure of sound in low strings lest the lowness descend to inaudibility, and a measure of tenseness in high strings lest they be broken by the thinness of the sound, being too tense, and all is congruous and fitting, so we perceive that in the music of the universe nothing can be excessive and destroy some other part by its own excess, but each part brings its own contribution or aids others to bring theirs. For what winter binds, spring releases, summer heats, autumn ripens; and the seasons in turn bring forth their own fruits or help the others to bring forth theirs. These matters will be discussed more searchingly later on.

What human music is, anyone may understand by examining his own nature. For what is that which unites the incorporeal activity of the reason with the body, unless it be a certain mutual adaptation and as it were a tempering of low and high sounds into a single consonance? What else joins together the parts of the soul itself, which in the opinion of Aristotle is a joining together of the rational and the irrational? [10] What causes the blending of the body's elements or holds its parts together in established adaptation? But of this I shall treat later.

The third kind of music is that which is described as residing in certain instruments. This is produced by tension, as in strings, or by blowing, as in the tibiae or in those instruments activated by water, or by some kind of percussion, as in instruments which are struck upon certain bronze concavities, by which means various sounds are produced.

It seems best in this work to treat first of the music of instruments. But enough of introduction. The elements of music themselves must now be discussed.

· · · · ·

33. WHAT A MUSICIAN IS

This is now to be considered: that every art, and every discipline as well, has by nature a more honorable character than a handicraft, which is produced by the hand and labor of a craftsman. For it is far greater and nobler to know what someone does than to accomplish oneself what someone else knows, for physical skill obeys like a handmaid while reason rules like a mistress. And unless the hand does what the mind sanctions, it is vain. How much more admirable, then, is the science of music in apprehending by reason than in accomplishing by work and deed! As much more so, namely, as the body is surpassed by the mind, because the person destitute of reason has lived in servitude. But reason rules and leads to the right. For unless its rule is obeyed, the work destitute of reason will waver. Thus it is that reason's contemplation of working does not need the deed, while the works of our hands are nothing unless led

10 *On the Soul,* 423A.

by reason. And how great the glory and merit of reason are can be understood from this: that the remaining physical craftsmen (so to speak) take their names, not from their discipline, but rather from their instruments. For the player of the cithara is so called from the cithara, the player of the aulos from the tibia, and the others from the names of their instruments. He however is a musician who on reflection has taken to himself the science of singing, not by the servitude of work but by the rule of contemplation—a thing that we see in the work of buildings and wars, namely in the opposite conferring of the name. For the buildings are inscribed and the triumphs held in the names of those by whose rule and reason they were begun, not of those by whose labor and servitude they were completed.

Thus there are three classes concerned with the musical art. One class has to do with instruments, another invents songs, a third judges the work of instruments and the song. But that class which is dedicated to instruments and there consumes its entire efforts, as for example the players of the cithara and those who show their skill on the organ and other musical instruments, are separated from the intellect of musical science, since they are servants, as has been said, nor do they bear anything of reason, being wholly destitute of speculation. The second class having to do with music is that of the poets, which is borne to song not so much by speculation and reason as by a certain natural instinct. Thus this class also is to be separated from music. The third is that which assumes the skill of judging, so that it weighs rhythms and melodies and the whole of song. And seeing that the whole is founded in reason and speculation, this class is rightly reckoned as musical, and that man as a musician who possesses the faculty of judging, according to speculation or reason, appropriate and suitable to music, of modes and rhythms and of the classes of melodies and their mixtures and of all those things about which there is to be discussion later on and of the songs of the poets.

12. Cassiodorus

Flavius Magnus Aurelius Cassiodorus was born at Scyllacium, in Lucania, about 485 A.D. He first occupied a distinguished position at the court of Theodoric and Athalaric, kings of the Ostrogoths, and later retired into the monastery at Vivarium which he had founded and developed into a center of learning. There he wrote his *Institutiones*, which contains a section on music written between 550 and 562.

Cassiodorus is one of the most important early writers on music and, with Boethius, one of the two great intermediaries between the music of the ancient world and that of the Middle Ages.

From the Institutiones [1]

5. OF MUSIC

1. A CERTAIN Gaudentius, writing of music, says that Pythagoras found its beginning in the sound of hammers and the striking of stretched strings.[2] Our friend Mutianus, a man of the greatest learning, has translated the work of Gaudentius in a manner attesting his skill. Clement of Alexandria in his *Exhortation to the Greeks* declares that music received its origin from the Muses, and takes pains to make clear for what reason the Muses themselves were invented: they were so named ἀπὸ τοῦ μῶσθαι, that is, from inquiring, because, as the ancients would have it, they were the first to inquire into the power of songs and the modulation of the voice.[3] We find also that Censorinus, in his treatise *De die natali*, addressed to Quintus Cerellius, has written things not to be overlooked

---

1 Text: As edited by R. A. B. Mynors for the Clarendon Press (Oxford, 1937), pp. 142–150.
2 *Eisagoge* (Meibom, pp. 13–15).
8 (ii, p. 65 in G. W. Butterworth's translation for the Loeb Classical Library). Clement reports that Alcman derived the origin of the Muses from Zeus and Mnemosyne; he does not speak of the origin of music. As for the etymology ἀπὸ τοῦ μῶσθαι, this is due to Plato, *Cratylus,* 406A.

concerning musical discipline, or the second part of mathematics,[4] for which reason it is profitable to read him, in order to implant those things more deeply in the mind by frequent meditation.

2. The discipline of music is diffused through all the actions of our life. First, it is found that if we perform the commandments of the Creator and with pure minds obey the rules he has laid down, every word we speak, every pulsation of our veins, is related by musical rhythms to the powers of harmony. Music indeed is the knowledge of apt modulation. If we live virtuously, we are constantly proved to be under its discipline, but when we commit injustice we are without music. The heavens and the earth, indeed all things in them which are directed by a higher power, share in this discipline of music, for Pythagoras attests that this universe was founded by and can be governed by music.

3. Music is closely bound up with religion itself. Witness the decachord of the Ten Commandments, the tinkling of the harp, the timbrel, the melody of the organ, the sound of cymbals.[5] The very Psalter is without doubt named after a musical instrument because the exceedingly sweet and grateful melody of the celestial virtues is contained within it.

4. Let us now discuss the parts of music, as it has been handed down from the elders. Musical science is the discipline which treats of numbers in their relation to those things which are found in sounds, such as duple, triple, quadruple, and others called relative that are similar to these.[6]

5. The parts of music are three: harmonics, rhythmics, metrics.[7]

Harmonics is the musical science which distinguishes the high and low in sounds.

Rhythmics is that which inquires whether words in combination sound well or badly together.

---

4 xiii, 1.

5 Cf. Psalm 150: 3-5.

6 *Musica scientia est disciplina quae de numeris loquitur qui ad aliquid sunt his qui inveniuntur in sonis, ut duplum, triplum, quadruplum, et his similia quae dicuntur ad aliquid.* This definition is designed to indicate the relation of music to the other divisions of mathematics and is an expansion of one which Cassiodorus has already given (II, iii, § 21) in introducing the subject of the quadrivium. "Mathematical science (or, as we may call it in Latin, 'doctrinal' science) is that science which considers abstract quantity. By abstract quantity we mean that quantity which we treat in a purely speculative way, separating it intellectually from its material and from its other accidents, such as evenness, oddness, and the like. It has these divisions: arithmetic, music, geometry, astronomy. Arithmetic is the discipline of absolute numerable quantity. Music is the discipline which treats of numbers in their relation to those things which are found in sounds. Geom-

etry is the discipline of immobile magnitude and of forms. Astronomy is the discipline of the course of the heavenly bodies; it contemplates all figures and with searching reason considers the orbits of the stars about themselves and about the earth." Compare Boethius, *De institutione arithmetica,* I, i: "Arithmetical impartiality inquires into absolute multitude; the continence of musical modulation investigates relative multitude; geometry declares the knowledge of immobile magnitude; the competence of astronomical discipline lays claim to the science of mobile magnitude." From these definitions by Cassiodorus and Boethius is derived the terse definition usual in the later Middle Ages: *Musica est de numero relato ad sonos*—Music has to do with number as related to sounds.

7 For this classification see Lasus of Hermione, as quoted by Martianus Capella (Meibom, p. 181-182) and Aristides Quintilianus (Meibom, p. 8), also Plutarch, *De musica,* 1142D, as emended by Reinach.

Metrics is that which by valid reasoning knows the measures of the various metres; for example, the heroic, the iambic, the elegiac.

6. There are three classes of musical instruments: instruments of percussion, instruments of tension, wind instruments.

Instruments of percussion comprise cup-shaped vessels of bronze and silver, or others whose hard metal, when struck, yields an agreeable clanging.

Instruments of tension are constructed with strings, held in place according to the rules of the art, which upon being struck by the plectrum delightfully soothe the ear. These comprise the various species of cithara.

Wind instruments are those which are actuated to produce a vocal sound when filled by a stream of air, as trumpets, reeds, organs, pandoria, and others of this nature.

7. We have still to explain about the symphonies.[8] Symphony is the fusion of a low sound with a high one or of a high sound with a low one, an adaptation effected either vocally or by blowing or striking. There are six symphonies:

1) diatessaron	4) diapason and diatessaron together
2) diapente	5) diapason and diapente together
3) diapason	6) disdiapason

I. The consonance diatessaron results from the ratio 4:3 (epitrita) and includes four sounds, hence its name.

II. The consonance diapente results from the ratio 3:2 (emiola) and includes five sounds.

III. The consonance diapason, also called diocto, results from the ratio 2:1 (diplasia or dupla) and includes eight sounds, hence also the name it takes of diocto or diapason—since the citharas of the ancients had eight strings this consonance, including as it does all sounds, is called diapason (literally, through all).[9]

IV. The consonance diapason and diatessaron together results from the ratio which the number 24 has to the number 8 [10] and includes eleven sounds.

V. The consonance diapason and diapente together results from the ratio 3:1 (triplasia) and includes twelve sounds.

VI. The consonance disdiapason, that is double diapason, results from the ratio 4:1 (tetraplasia) and includes fifteen sounds.

---

8 This account of the "symphonies" is drawn largely from Gaudentius, *Eisagoge* (Meibom, pp. 11–13).

9 This is of course an incorrect explanation. Compare the pseudo-Aristotelian *Problems*, xix, 32 (920A): "Why is the octave called the 'diapason' instead of being called the diocto according to the number of the notes, in the same way as the terms used for the fourth and fifth? Is it because originally there were seven strings? Then Terpander took away the trite and added the nete, and at that time it was called the diapason, not the diocto, for there were seven notes." (From the translation by W. S. Hett for the Loeb Classical Library)

10 The correct ratio is 24:9, or 8:3.

8. Key is a difference or quantity of the whole harmonic system, consisting in the intonation or level of the voice. There are fifteen keys:

Hypodorian	Dorian	Hyperdorian
Hypoiastian	Iastian	Hyperiastian
Hypophrygian	Phrygian	Hyperphrygian
Hypoaeolian	Aeolian	Hyperaeolian
Hypolydian	Lydian	Hyperlydian

I. The Hypodorian key is the one sounding lowest of all, for which reason it is also called lower.

II. The Hypoiastian exceeds the Hypodorian by a semitone.

III. The Hypophrygian exceeds the Hypoiastian by a semitone, the Hypodorian by a tone.

IV. The Hypoaeolian exceeds the Hypophrygian by a semitone, the Hypoiastian by a tone, the Hypodorian by a tone and a half.

V. The Hypolydian exceeds the Hypoaeolian by a semitone, the Hypophrygian by a tone, the Hypoiastian by a tone and a half, the Hypodorian by two tones.

VI. The Dorian exceeds the Hypolydian by a semitone, the Hypoaeolian by a tone, the Hypophrygian by a tone and a half, the Hypoiastian by two tones, the Hypodorian by two tones and a half, that is, by the consonance diatessaron.

VII. The Iastian exceeds the Dorian by a semitone, the Hypolydian by a tone, the Hypoaeolian by a tone and a half, the Hypophrygian by two tones, the Hypoiastian by two tones and a half, that is, by the consonance diatessaron, the Hypodorian by three tones.

VIII. The Phrygian exceeds the Iastian by a semitone, the Dorian by a tone, the Hypolydian by a tone and a half, the Hypoaeolian by two tones, the Hypophrygian by two tones and a half, that is, by the consonance diatessaron, the Hypoiastian by three tones, the Hypodorian by three tones and a half, that is, by the consonance diapente.

IX. The Aeolian exceeds the Phrygian by a semitone, the Iastian by a tone, the Dorian by a tone and a half, the Hypolydian by two tones, the Hypoaeolian by two tones and a half, that is, by the consonance diatessaron, the Hypophrygian by three tones, the Hypoiastian by three tones and a half, that is, by the consonance diapente, the Hypodorian by four tones.

X. The Lydian exceeds the Aeolian by a semitone, the Phrygian by a tone, the Iastian by a tone and a half, the Dorian by two tones, the Hypolydian by two tones and a half, that is, by the consonance diatessaron, the Hypoaeolian by three tones, the Hypophrygian by three tones and a half, that is, by the consonance diapente, the Hypoiastian by four tones, the Hypodorian by four tones and a half.

XI. The Hyperdorian exceeds the Lydian by a semitone, the Aeolian by a tone, the Phrygian by a tone and a half, the Iastian by two tones, the Dorian by two tones and a half, that is, by the consonance diatessaron, the Hypolydian by three tones, the Hypoaeolian by three tones and a half, that is, by the consonance diapente, the Hypophrygian by four tones, the Hypoiastian by four tones and a half, the Hypodorian by five tones.

XII. The Hyperiastian exceeds the Hyperdorian by a semitone, the Lydian by a tone, the Aeolian by a tone and a half, the Phrygian by two tones, the Iastian by two tones and a half, that is, by the consonance diatessaron, the Dorian by three tones, the Hypolydian by three tones and a half, that is, by the consonance diapente, the Hypoaeolian by four tones, the Hypophrygian by four tones and a half, the Hypoiastian by five tones, the Hypodorian by five tones and a half.

XIII. The Hyperphrygian exceeds the Hyperiastian by a semitone, the Hyperdorian by a tone, the Lydian by a tone and a half, the Aeolian by two tones, the Phrygian by two tones and a half, that is, by the consonance diatessaron, the Iastian by three tones, the Dorian by three tones and a half, that is, by the consonance diapente, the Hypolydian by four tones, the Hypoaeolian by four tones and a half, the Hypophrygian by five tones, the Hypoiastian by five tones and a half, the Hypodorian by six tones, that is, by the consonance diapason.

XIV. The Hyperaeolian exceeds the Hyperphrygian by a semitone, the Hyperiastian by a tone, the Hyperdorian by a tone and a half, the Lydian by two tones, the Aeolian by two tones and a half, that is, by the consonance diatessaron, the Phrygian by three tones, the Iastian by three tones and a half, that is, by the consonance diapente, the Dorian by four tones, the Hypolydian by four tones and a half, the Hypoaeolian by five tones, the Hypophrygian by five tones and a half, the Hypoiastian by six tones, that is, by the consonance diapason, the Hypodorian by six tones and a half.

XV. The Hyperlydian, the newest and highest of all, exceeds the Hyperaeolian by a semitone, the Hyperphrygian by a tone, the Hyperiastian by a tone and a half, the Hyperdorian by two tones, the Lydian by two tones and a half, that is, by the consonance diatessaron, the Aeolian by three tones, the Phrygian by three tones and a half, that is, by the consonance diapente, the Iastian by four tones, the Dorian by four tones and a half, the Hypolydian by five tones, the Hypoaeolian by five tones and a half, the Hypophrygian by six tones, that is, by the consonance diapason, the Hypoiastian by six tones and a half, the Hypodorian by seven tones.

From this it appears that the Hyperlydian key, the highest of all, exceeds the Hypodorian, the lowest of all, by seven tones. So useful, Varro observes, is the virtue displayed in these keys that they can compose distraught minds and also attract the very beasts, even serpents, birds, and dolphins to listen to their melody.

9. But of the lyre of Orpheus and the songs of the Sirens, as being

fabulous matters, we shall say nothing. Yet what shall we say of David, who freed Saul from the unclean spirit by the discipline of most wholesome melody, and by a new method, through the sense of hearing, restored the king to the health which the physicians had been unable to bestow by the virtues of herbs? Asclepiades the physician, according to the ancients a most learned man, is recorded to have restored a man from frenzy to his former sanity by means of melody. Many other miracles have been wrought upon the sick by this discipline. It is said that the heavens themselves, as we have recalled above, are made to revolve by sweet harmony. And to embrace all in a few words, nothing in things celestial or terrestrial which is fittingly conducted according to the Creator's own plan is found to be exempt from this discipline.

10. This study, therefore, which both lifts up our sense to celestial things and pleases our ears with melody, is most grateful and useful. Among the Greeks Alypius, Euclid, Ptolemy, and others have written excellent treatises on the subject. Of the Romans the distinguished Albinus has treated it with compendious brevity. We recall obtaining his book in a library in Rome and reading it with zeal. If this work has been carried off in consequence of the barbarian invasion, you have here the Latin version of Gaudentius by Mutianus; if you read this with close attention it will open to you the courts of this science. It is said that Apuleius of Madaura has also brought together the doctrines of this work in Latin speech. Also St. Augustine, a father of the church, wrote in six books *De musica*, in which he showed that human speech naturally has rhythmical sounds and a measured harmony in its long and short syllables. Censorinus also has treated with subtlety of the accents of our speech, declaring that they have a relation to musical discipline. Of this book, along with others, I have left a transcript with you.

13. Isidore of Seville

Born in Cartagena ("New Carthage," in southeastern Spain), Isidore was brought to Seville in early childhood and in 599 succeeded his brother Leander as archbishop of that city; he died in 636. Teacher, administrator, controversialist, and scholar, he made important contributions to chronology and historiography and, in his *Etymologiarum sive originum libri xx*, written between 622 and 633, compiled an encyclopaedic treatise on the arts and sciences in the form of an inquiry into the origins of their technical terms. In addition to the chapters which follow, devoted exclusively to music, Isidore's treatise also includes a chapter on the Divine Offices (VI, xix), with many definitions of interest to the student of liturgical music. Like Boethius and Cassiodorus, Isidore was one of those intermediaries from whose writings the early Middle Ages derived their impressions of the ancient world.

From the Etymologiarum [1]

Book Three

15. OF MUSIC AND ITS NAME

MUSIC IS an art of modulation consisting of tone and song, called music by derivation from the Muses. The Muses were so named ἀπὸ τοῦ μῶσθαι, that is from inquiring, because, as the ancients would have it, they inquired into the power of songs and the modulation of the voice. The sound of these, since it is an impression upon the sense, flows by into the past and is imprinted upon the memory. Hence it was fabled by the poets that the Muses were the daughters of Jove and Memory. Unless sounds are remembered by man, they perish, for they cannot be written down. [2]

---

1 Text: As edited by W. M. Lindsay for the Clarendon Press (Oxford, 1911).

2 Cf. St. Augustine, *De ordine*, II, xiv: "And since what the intellect perceives (and numbers

16. OF ITS INVENTORS

Moses says that the inventor of the art of music was Tubal, who was of the race of Cain, before the flood.[3] The Greeks say that Pythagoras found its beginnings in the sound of hammers and the striking of stretched strings. Others report that Linus the Theban and Zetus and Amphion were the first to become illustrious in musical art. After their time this discipline gradually came to be especially ordered and was expanded in many ways, and not to know music was as disgraceful as to be unlettered. It was not only introduced into sacred rites, but was used in all festivals and on all joyful or mournful occasions. For as hymns were sung in the worship of the gods, so hymenaeal songs were sung at weddings, and threnodies and lamentations to the sound of tibiae at funerals. At banquets the lyre or the cithara was passed from hand to hand, and festal songs were assigned to each guest in turn.

17. WHAT MUSIC CAN DO

Thus without music no discipline can be perfect, for there is nothing without it. For the very universe, it is said, is held together by a certain harmony of sounds, and the heavens themselves are made to revolve by the modulation of harmony. Music moves the feelings and changes the emotions. In battles, moreover, the sound of the trumpet rouses the combatants, and the more furious the trumpeting, the more valorous their spirit. Song likewise encourages the rowers, music soothes the mind to endure toil, and the modulation of the voice consoles the weariness of each labor. Music also composes distraught minds, as may be read of David, who freed Saul from the unclean spirit by the art of melody. The very beasts also, even serpents, birds, and dolphins, music incites to listen to her melody. But every word we speak, every pulsation of our veins, is related by musical rhythms to the powers of harmony.

18. OF THE THREE PARTS OF MUSIC

The parts of music are three: that is, harmonics, rhythmics, metrics. Harmonics is that which distinguishes the high and low in sounds. Rhythmics is that which inquires whether words in combination sound well or badly together. Metrics is that which by valid reasoning knows the

---

are manifestly of this class) is always of the present and is deemed immortal, while sound, since it is an impression upon the sense, flows by into the past and is imprinted upon the memory, Reason has permitted the poets to pretend, in a reasonable fable, that the Muses were the daugh-

ters of Jove and Memory. Hence this discipline, which addresses itself to the intellect and to the sense alike, has acquired the name of Music." From Isidore's concluding sentence it is clear that he has only partly understood his authority.

3 Genesis 4:21.

measures of the various metres; for example, the heroic, the iambic, the elegiac.

19. OF THE THREEFOLD DIVISION OF MUSIC

Moreover for every sound which forms the material of songs, there is a threefold nature. The first is the harmonic, which consists of singing; the second, the organic, which is produced by blowing; the third, the rhythmic, in which the music is produced by the impulse of the fingers. For sound is caused either by the voice, as with the throat, or by blowing, as with the trumpet or the tibia, or by an impulse, as with the cithara or with anything else which becomes resonant when struck.[4]

20. OF THE FIRST DIVISION OF MUSIC, CALLED HARMONIC

The first division of music, which is called the harmonic, that is, the modulation of the voice, is the affair of comedians, tragedians, and choruses and of all who sing. It produces motion of the mind and body, and from this motion sound. From this sound comes the music which in man is called voice.

Voice is air struck (*verberatus*) by the breath, from which circumstance words (*verba*) also receive their name. Voice is proper to man and to irrational animals. For sound in other things is called voice by a misuse and not properly, as, "The voice of the trumpet snarled," and

Broken voices by the shore.[5]

For the proper locutions are that the cliffs of the shore should resound, and

The trumpet with resonant brass a terrible sound afar
Gave forth.[6]

Harmony is a modulation of the voice and a concordance or mutual adaptation of several sounds.

Symphony is a fusion of the modulation of low and high concordant sounds, produced either vocally or by blowing or striking. Through symphony low and high sounds are concordant, in such a way that if any one of them is dissonant it offends the sense of hearing. The opposite of this is diaphony, that is, discrepant or dissonant sounds.

---

4 Cf. St. Augustine, *De ordine*, II, xiv: "Reason has understood that the judgment of the ear has to do only with sound and that sound has three varieties: it consists either in the voice of an animate being, or in what blowing produces in instruments, or in what is brought forth by striking. The first variety it understands to be the affair of tragedians, comedians, choruses, and the like, and in general of all who sing. The second it understands to be allotted to the auloi and similar instruments. To the third it understands to be given the citharas, lyres, cymbals, and anything else which becomes resonant when struck."

5 Vergil, *Aeneid*, iii, 556.

6 *Ibid.*, ix, 503.

Euphony is sweetness of the voice; it is also called melody, from the word *mel* (honey), because of its sweetness.

Diastema is an interval of the voice composed of two or more sounds.

Diesis consists of certain intervals and diminutions of modulation and interpolations between one sound and another.

Key is a raised enunciation of the voice. For it is a difference and quantity of the harmony consisting in the intonation or level of the voice, of which musicians have divided the varieties into fifteen parts, of which the Hyperlydian is the newest and highest, and the Hypodorian the lowest of all.

Song is an inflecting of the voice, for sound is simple and moreover it precedes song.

Arsis is a lifting up of the voice, that is, a beginning.

Thesis is a lowering of the voice, that is, an end.

Sweet voices are fine, full, loud, and high.

Penetrating voices are those which can hold a note an unusually long time, in such a way that they continuously fill the whole place, like the sound of trumpets.

A thin voice is one lacking in breath, as the voice of children or women or the sick. This is as it is in strings, for the finest strings emit fine, thin sounds.

In fat voices, as those of men, much breath is emitted at once.

A sharp voice is high and thin, as we see in strings.

A hard voice is one which emits sound violently, like thunder, like the sound of an anvil whenever the hammer is struck against the hard iron.

A harsh voice is a hoarse one, which is broken up by minute, dissimilar impulses.

A blind voice is one which is choked off as soon as produced, and once silent cannot be prolonged, as in crockery.

A pretty (*vinnola*) voice is soft and flexible; it is so called from *vinnus*, a softly curling lock of hair.

The perfect voice is high, sweet, and loud: high, to be adequate to the sublime; loud, to fill the ear; sweet, to soothe the minds of the hearers. If any one of these qualities is absent, the voice is not perfect.

21. OF THE SECOND DIVISION OF MUSIC, CALLED ORGANIC

The second division is the organic, found in the instruments which are activated to produce a vocal sound when filled by a stream of air, such as trumpets, reeds, pipes, organs, pandoria, and similar instruments.

Organ is the generic name of all musical vessels. The Greeks have another name for the kind of organ to which bellows are applied, but their common custom is to call it the organ.

The trumpet was invented by the Etruscans. Virgil writes:

> And Etruscan clangor of trumpets seemed to resound
> Through the air.[7]

It was employed not only in battles, but in all festivals of special praise-giving or rejoicing. Wherefore it is also said in the Psalter: [8] "Sound the trumpet at the beginning of the month, and on the day of your great solemnity." For the Jews were commanded to sound the trumpet at the time of the new moon, as they still do.

The tibiae, according to report, were devised in Phrygia. They were long used only in funerals, and afterward in the sacred rites of the heathen. It is thought that they are called tibiae because they were first made from the leg-bones of deer and fawns, and that then, by a misuse of the term, the name was used of those not made of leg-bones. Hence it is also called *tibicen*, as if for *tibiae cantus* (song of the leg-bone).

The reed is rightly the name of a tree, called *calamus* from *calendo*, that is, giving out voice.

The pipe some think to have been invented by Mercury; others, by Faunus, whom the Greeks call Pan; some by Daphnis, a shepherd of Agrigentum in Sicily. The pipe (*fistula*) is also named from sending forth a sound, for in Greek voice is called φώς, and sent forth, στόλια.

The sambuca, among musicians, is a kind of drum. The word means a kind of fragile wood, from which tibiae are made.

The pandoria is named from its inventor, of whom Virgil says:

> Pan first taught men to join reeds together with wax;
> Pan cares for sheep and shepherds.[9]

For among the heathen he was the god of shepherds, who first adapted reeds of unequal length to music and fitted them together with studious art.

22. OF THE THIRD DIVISION OF MUSIC, WHICH IS CALLED RHYTHMIC

The third division is the rhythmic, having to do with strings and striking, to which are assigned the different species of cithara, also the tympanum, the cymbal, the sistrum, vessels of bronze and silver, or

---

7 *Ibid.*, viii, 526.
8 Psalm 81:3.
9 *Eclogues*, ii, 32.

others whose hard metal, when struck, yields an agreeable clanging, and other instruments of this nature.

Tubal, as was said before, is regarded as the inventor of the cithara and psaltery, but by the Greeks Apollo was believed to have first discovered the use of the cithara. According to their tradition, the form of the cithara was originally like that of the human chest, because it gives forth sound as the chest gives forth voice, and it received its name from that reason, for in Doric the chest was called κιθάρα. Gradually numerous species were invented, as psalteries, lyres, barbitae, phoenices, and pectides, and those which are called Indian citharae and are played by two musicians at once; also many others, some of square and others of triangular form. The number of strings was also increased and the type altered. The ancients called the cithara *fidicula* and *fidicen,* because the strings are in good accord with each other, as befits men among whom there is trust (*fides*).

The ancient cithara had seven strings; whence Virgil's phrase, "the seven distinctions of sounds"; [10] "distinctions" because no string gives the same note as its neighbor. The strings were seven because that number filled the range of the voice, or because the heavens sound with seven motions. The strings (*chordae*) are so called from *cor* (heart), because the striking of the strings of the cithara is like the beating of the heart in the breast. Mercury was their inventor, and he was the first to compel sound to reside in strings.

The psaltery, popularly called *canticum,* has its name from *psallendo* (singing), because the chorus answers its voice in consonance. It resembles a barbaric cithara in the form of the letter delta, but there is this difference between it and the cithara, that it has its wooden sound-box above, and the strings are struck below and sound above, while the cithara has the sound-box below. The Hebrews used a ten-stringed psaltery, because of the ten commandments of their law.

The lyre is so called ἀπὸ τοῦ ληρεῖν (from sounding folly), that is, from the variety of voices, because it produces dissimilar sounds. They say it was invented by Mercury in the following manner. When the Nile, retreating into its channels, had left various animals in the fields, a tortoise was left behind. When it had putrefied and its sinews remained stretched within its shell, it gave out a sound on being struck by Mercury. After this pattern he made the lyre and transmitted it to Orpheus, who applied himself studiously to it and is deemed not merely to have swayed wild beasts with this art, but to have moved rocks and forests with the modulation of his song. Musicians have feigned in their fables that the

---

[10] *Aeneid.* vi, 646.

Lyre was placed among the constellations because of his love of study and the glory of his song.

The tympanum is a skin or hide stretched over one side of a wooden frame; it is a half-drum, shaped like a sieve. It is called tympanum because it is a half, for which reason a half-pearl is called a tympanum. It is struck with a stick as a drum is.

Cymbals are certain vessels which produce sound when struck together. They are called cymbals because they are struck together in time with dancing, since the Greeks call dancing συμβαλεῖν.

The sistrum is named from its inventress, for Isis, a queen of the Egyptians, is considered to have invented this species of instrument. Juvenal has:

Let Isis with angry sistrum blind my eyes.[11]

Women use this instrument because a woman invented it. So among the Amazons the army of women was summoned by the sistrum.

The bell (*tintinnabulum*) is named from its sound, as are also the clapping (*plausus*) of hands and the creaking (*stridor*) of hinges.

Drum (*symphonia*) is the ordinary name of a wooden frame covered on both sides with stretched skin, which the musicians strike in one place and another with small sticks, and there results a most delightful sound from the concord of low and high.

23. OF MUSICAL NUMBERS

You obtain musical numbers in this manner. Having set down the extreme terms, as say 6 and 12, you see by how many units 12 exceeds 6, and it is by 6 units. You square this: 6 times 6 is 36. You then add together those first extremes, 6 and 12; together they make 18. You then divide 36 by 18, which gives 2. Add this to the smaller number, that is, 6; this will give 8, and it will be the harmonic mean between 6 and 12.[12]

From this it appears that 8 exceeds 6 by 2 units, that is, by one-third of 6, and 8 is exceeded by 12 by 4 units, one-third of 12. By the same fraction that it exceeds, it is exceeded.

But just as this ratio appears in the universe from the revolution of the

---

11 *Satires*, xiii, 931.

12 This method for finding the harmonic mean between two extremes will give the correct answer only when the greater term is twice the lesser. Isidore's error lies in directing that the difference between the extremes be squared. It must be multiplied by the lesser term. With this correction his method agrees with that given by Boethius, *De institutione musica*, II, xvii: "If we

seek the harmonic mean, we add the extremes, for example 10 and 40, one to another, making 50. Their difference, which is 30, we multiply by the lesser term, that is 10, making 10 times 30, or 300. This we divide by 50, making 6. This we add to the lesser term, making 16. If now we place this number between 10 and 40, we have a harmonic proportion."

spheres, so in the microcosm it is so inexpressibly potent that the man without its perfection and deprived of harmony does not exist. And by the perfection of the same music, measures consist of arsis and thesis, that is, of raising and lowering.

IV

Musical Theory in the Middle Ages

14. Odo of Cluny

A writer of the tenth century and a pupil of Remi (Remigius) of Auxerre, St. Odo of Cluny was in 899 canon and choir-singer at St. Martin of Tours and later became abbot of various French monasteries. In 927 he became head of the famous abbey of Cluny, where he died in 942.

Odo is credited with a number of important writings on the theory of music, among them the *Enchiridion musices*, also called *Dialogus de musica*. The *Enchiridion* contains the first systematic use of letters for pitches in the meaning that was to become standard for the Middle Ages—the full gamut extending from A to g, with the addition of the low Γ and the high a'.

Enchiridion musices

[*ca. 935*]

A book, also called a dialogue, composed by Dom Odo and concisely, properly, and becomingly brought together for the benefit of readers.[1]

PROLOGUE

You HAVE insistently requested, beloved brothers, that I should communicate to you a few rules concerning music, these to be only of a sort which boys and simple persons may understand and by means of which, with God's help, they may quickly attain to perfect skill in singing. You asked this, having yourselves seen and heard and by sure evidence verified that it could be done. For indeed, being stationed among you, with God's help alone I taught certain actual boys and youths by means of this art so that some after three days, others after four days, and one after a single week of training in it, were able to learn several antiphons and in a short

1 Text: Gerbert, *Scriptores*, I, 251–259, 263–264. There is a German translation by Bohn in *Monatshefte für Musik-Geschichte*, XII (1880), No. 2–3.

time to sing them without hesitation, not hearing them sung by anyone, but contenting themselves simply with a copy written according to the rules. With the passage of not many days they were singing at first sight and extempore and without a fault anything written in music, something which until now ordinary singers had never been able to do, many continuing to practice and study singing for fifty years without profit.

When you were earnestly and diligently inquiring whether our doctrines would be of value for all melodies, taking as my helper a certain brother who seemed perfect in comparison with other singers, I investigated the Antiphoner of the blessed Gregory, in which I found that nearly all things were regularly set down. A few things, corrupted by unskilled singers, were corrected, both on the evidence of other singers and by the authority of the rules. But in the longer melodies, beloved brothers, we found sounds belonging to the high modes and excessive ascents and descents, contrary to the rule. Yet, since universal usage agreed in defending these melodies, we did not presume to emend them. We noted them as unusual, however, in order that no one inquiring into the truth of the rule might be left in doubt.

This done, you were kindled by a greater desire and insisted, with vehement entreaties and urgings, not only that rules should be made, but also that the whole Antiphoner should be written in useful notes and with the formulas of the tones,[2] to the honor of God and of His Most Holy Mother Mary, in whose venerable monastery these things were being done.

Deriving confidence, therefore, from your entreaties, and complying with the orders of our common father, I am neither willing nor able to discontinue this work. For among the learned of this age the doctrine of this art is very difficult and extensive. Let therefore whoever pleases cultivate the field further with unwilling labor and wall it in. He who of himself perceives this little gift of God will be satisfied with a simple fruit. And in order that this may be the better understood and that you may receive what is necessary in proportion to your true desire, let one of you come forward to converse or ask questions. These I shall not neglect to answer, in so far as the Lord has given me the power.

---

2 For the formulas of the tones—"Primum quaerite regnum Dei," "Secundem autem simile est huic," and so forth—see Dom Pothier, *Les mélodies grégoriennes* (Solesmes, 1881), p. 289-290, or W. H. Frere in *Grove's Dictionary of Music and Musicians*, 3rd ed., III (London, 1928), 481. Odo's reference to these formulas indicates that the Antiphoner of which he speaks will have been provided with a Tonarius or classified list of the antiphons and responds, arranged according to the eight modes and sub-arranged according to their differences.

1. OF THE MONOCHORD AND ITS USE

(Disciple) What is music?

(Master) The science of singing truly and the easy road to perfection in singing.

(D) How so?

(M) As the teacher first shows you all the letters in a table, so the musician introduces all the sounds of melody on the monochord.

(D) What is the monochord?

(M) It is a long rectangular wooden chest, hollow within like a cithara; upon it is mounted a string, by the sounding of which you easily understand the varieties of sounds.

(D) How is the string itself mounted?

(M) A straight line is drawn down the middle of the chest, length-wise, and points are marked on the line at a distance of one inch from each end. In the spaces outside these points two end-pieces are set, which hold the string so suspended above the line that the line beneath the string is of the same length as the string between the two end-pieces.

(D) How does one string produce many different sounds?

(M) The letters, or notes, used by musicians are placed in order on the line beneath the string, and when the bridge is moved between the line and the string, shortening or lengthening it, the string marvelously reproduces each melody by means of these letters. When any antiphon is marked with the same letters, the boys learn it better and more easily from the string than if they heard some one sing it, and after a few months' training, they are able to discard the string and sing by sight alone, without hesitation, music that they have never heard.

(D) What you say is very marvelous. Our singers, indeed, have never aspired to such perfection.

(M) Instead, brother, they missed the right path, and failing to ask the way, they labored all their life in vain.

(D) How can it be true that a string teaches more than a man?

(M) A man sings as he will or can, but the string is divided with such art by very learned men, using the aforesaid letters, that if it is diligently observed or considered, it cannot mislead.

2. OF THE MEASUREMENT OF THE MONOCHORD

(D) What is this art, I inquire.

(M) The measurement of the monochord, for if it is well measured, it never deceives.

(D) Can I perchance learn the exact measurements, simply and in a few words?

(M) Today, with God's help; only listen diligently.

At the first end-piece of the monochord, at the point at which we have spoken above, place the letter Γ, that is, a Greek G. (This Γ, since it is a letter rarely used, is by many not understood.) Carefully divide the distance from Γ to the point placed at the other end into nine parts, and where the first ninth from Γ ends, write the letter A; we shall call this the first step. Then, similarly, divide the distance from the first letter, A, to the end into nine, and at the first ninth, place the letter B for the second step. Then return to the beginning, divide by four from Γ, and for the third step write the letter C. From the first letter, A, divide similarly by four, and for the fourth step, write the letter D. In the same way, dividing B by four, you will find the fifth step, E. The third letter, C, likewise reveals the sixth step, F. Then return to Γ, and from it and from the other letters that follow it in order, divide the line in two parts, that is, in the middle, until, without Γ, you have fourteen or fifteen steps.

When you divide the sounds in the middle, you must mark them differently. For example, when you bisect the distance from Γ, instead of Γ, write G; for A bisected, set down a second a; for B, a second ♮; for C, a second c; for D, a second d; for E, a second e; for F, a second f; for G, a second g; and for a, a second $_a^a$; so that from the middle of the monochord forward, the letters will be the same as in the first part.

In addition, from the sixth step, F, divide into four, and before ♮, place a second round b; these two are accepted as a single step, one being called the second ninth step, and both are not regularly found in the same melody.

The figures, moreover, both sounds and letters, are thus arranged in order:

	Γ		
First step	A	Eighth step	a
Second step	B	First ninth step	b
		Second ninth step	♮
Third step	C	Tenth step	c
Fourth step	D	Eleventh step	d
Fifth step	E	Twelfth step	e
Sixth step	F	Thirteenth step	f
Seventh step	G	Fourteenth step	g
		Fifteenth step	$_a^a$

(D) Thanks be to God, I understand well, and I am confident that I shall now know how to make a monochord.[3]

---

[3] A monochord made according to Odo's direc-tions will give the so-called Pythagorean intona-tion, the semitone (256/243) being obtained by subtracting the sum of two whole tones (9/8 plus 9/8 equals 81/64) from the fourth (4/3). Some-what differently worded, Odo's directions are given also by Guido in the *Micrologus* (GS, II, 4–5) and in the *Epistola de ignoto cantu* (GS,

3. OF TONE AND SEMITONE

But why is it, I entreat, that I see on the regularly measured mono-chord in one place smaller and in another place larger spaces and intervals between the steps?

(M) The greater space is called a tone; it is from Γ to the first step, A, and from the first step, A, to the second, B. The lesser space, such as that from the second step, B, to the third, C, is called a semitone and makes a more restricted rise and fall. By no measure or number may the space of a semitone amount to that of a tone, but when the divisions are made in their places by the ratio given above, tones and semitones are formed.

If you have marked all the steps to the last, you will marvel to find in all of them a ninefold division just as you found it at first from Γ to the first step, A, and from the first step, A, to the second, B. Yet the first and second ninth steps, b and ♮, form with respect to one another neither a tone nor a semitone, but from the first ninth step, b, to the eighth, a, is a semitone and to the tenth, c, a tone; conversely, from the second ninth step, ♮, to the eighth, a, is a tone and to the tenth, c, a semitone. Thus one of them is always superfluous, and in each melody you accept one and reject the other in order not to seem to be making a tone and a semitone in the same place, which would be absurd.

(D) It is most marvelous that, although I did not divide by nine, except from Γ to the first step, A, and from the first step, A, to the second, B, I have found that all the tones are equally based on a ninefold division. But show me, I pray you, whether there are other divisions of the mono-chord and whether they are found in all or in several places.

4. OF THE CONSONANCES

(M) Besides the division of the tone, there are three divisions which govern the natural position of sounds which I have mentioned above.

The first is the quaternary division, as from the first step, A, to the fourth, D, so called because it is a division by four; this has four pitches and three intervals, namely, two tones and one semitone. Therefore, wherever you find two tones and a semitone between two pitches on the monochord, you will discover on trial that the interval formed by these two pitches extends to the very end in quaternary division; for this reason it is called diatessaron, that is, "of four."

The second is the ternary division, as from the first step, A, to the

---

II, 46, here perhaps an interpolation). In the *Micrologus* and in the *Regulae rhythmicae* (GS, II, 26–27) Guido gives also a second method of obtaining the same results, quicker but more difficult to remember.

fifth, E, this contains five pitches and four intervals, namely, three tones and one semitone. Therefore, wherever you see three tones and one semitone between two pitches, the interval formed by these two pitches will extend to the end by successive divisions of one-third. This interval is called diapente, that is, "of five," because it encloses five pitches.

The third is what is divided by two, or in the middle; it is called diapason, that is, "of all." This, as was said above, you will plainly recognize from the likeness of the letters, as from the first step, A, to the eighth, a. It consists of eight pitches and seven intervals, namely, of five tones and two semitones, for it contains one diatessaron and one diapente, the interval from the first step, A, to the fourth, D, forming a diatessaron, that from the fourth step, D, to the eighth, a, forming a diapente. From the first step, A, to the eighth, a, the diapason is obtained in the following manner: A, B, C, D, E, F, G, a.

(D) In few words I have learned not a little about divisions. Now I wish to hear why the same letters are used both in the first and in the second part.

(M) The reason is, that since the sounds of the second part, beginning with the seventh step, G (but excepting the first ninth step, b), are formed from those of the first part by the diapason, both parts so agree with each other that whatever letters form a tone, semitone, diatessaron, diapente, or diapason in the first part will likewise be found to do so in the second part. For example, in the first part, from Γ to A is a tone, to B is a tone and a tone, that is, a ditone, to C a diatessaron, to D a diapente, to G a diapason; similarly, in the second part, from G to a is a tone, to ♮ is a tone and a tone, to c a diatessaron, to d a diapente, to g a diapason. From this it follows that every melody is similarly sung in the first and in the second part. But the sounds of the first part sound in concord with those of the second part, as men's voices with those of boys.

(D) I consider that this has been wisely done. Now I expect to hear first how I may note down a melody so that I may understand it without a teacher and so that, when you give me examples of the rules, I may recognize the melody better and, if anything completely escape my memory, have recourse to such notes with entire confidence.

(M) Place before your eyes the letters of the monochord as the melody ranges through them; then, if you do not fully recognize the force of the letters themselves, you may hear them and learn them, wonderful to relate, from a master without his knowing it.

(D) Indeed I say that you have given me a wonderful master, who, made by me, teaches me, and teaching me, knows nothing himself. Nay, for his patience and obedience I fervently embrace him, and he will never torment me with blows or abuse when provoked by the slowness of my sense.

(M) He is a good master, but he demands a diligent listener.

5. OF THE CONJUNCTIONS OF SOUNDS

(D) To what am I to direct especial diligence?

(M) To the conjunctions of sounds which form various consonances, so that, just as they are various and different, you may be able to pronounce each of them opportunely in a dissimilar and different manner.

(D) How many differences there are, I pray you to teach me and show me by examples in common use.

(M) There are six, both in descent and in ascent. The first conjunction of sounds is when we join two sounds between which there is one semitone, as from the fifth step, E, to the sixth, F, a consonance closer and more restricted than any other; for example, the first ascent of the Antiphon "Haec est quae nescivit" or, in descent, conversely, "Vidimus stellam." The second is when there is a tone between two sounds, as from the third step, C, to the fourth, D; in ascent: "Non vos relinquam" and in descent: "Angelus Domini." The third is when a tone and a semitone make the difference between two sounds, as between the fourth step, D, and the sixth, F; in ascent: "Joannes autem" and in descent: "In lege." The fourth is when between one sound and another there are two tones, as from the sixth step, F, to the eighth, a; in ascent: "Adhuc multa habeo" and in descent: "Ecce Maria." The fifth is by means of a diatessaron, as from the first step, A, to the fourth, D; in ascent: "Valde honorandus" and in descent: "Secundum autem." The sixth is by means of a diapente, as from the fourth step, D, to the eighth, a, thus: "Primum quaerite," or, in descent, from the seventh step, G, to the third, C, thus: "Canite tuba." [4] Other regular conjunctions of sounds are nowhere found.

Haec est quae ne-sci-vit

Vi-di-mus stel-lam e-jus

---

[4] In Gerbert's edition, the beginnings of the various melodies cited in this chapter are printed (often very incorrectly) in small and capital letters, immediately above their opening words. These illustrations are here replaced by incipits copied from the Vatican edition of the Antiphoner, from the Tonarius in Vol. 9 of the *Paléographie musicale*, and from Dom Pothier's *Les Mélodies grégoriennes* (Solesmes, 1881).

Non vos re-lin-quam

An-ge-lus Do-mi-ni nun-ti-a-vit

Jo-han-nes au-tem cum au-dis-set

In le-ge Do-mi-ni

Ad-huc mul-ta ha-be-o

Ec-ce Ma-ri-a ge-nu-it

Val-de ho-no-ran-dus est

Se-cun-dum au-tem si-mi-le est hu-ic

Pri-mum quae-ri-te re-gnum De-i

Ca-ni-te tu-ba in Sy-on

6. OF THE DISTINGUISHING OF TONE AND SEMITONE ACCORDING TO
THE MODES

Ordinary singers often fall into the greatest error because they scarcely
consider the force of tone and semitone and of the other consonances. Each
of them chooses what first pleases his ear or appears easiest to utter or
to pronounce, and with many melodies a great error is made in the mode.
(I use the term "mode" of all the eight tones and modes of all melodies
composed in the formulas in order, for if I said "tone," it would be un-
certain whether I was speaking of the tones of the formulas or of the tones

formed by nine-fold disposition and division.) These singers, if you question them about the mode of any melody, promptly answer what they do not know as though they knew it perfectly. But if you ask them how they know it, they say falteringly: "Because at the beginning and end it is like other melodies of the same mode," although they do not know the mode of any melody at all. They do not know that a dissimilarity in a single sound forces the mode to change, as in the Antiphon "O beatum Pontificem," which, although in the second mode at the beginning and end, was most painstakingly emended to the first mode by Dom Odo, merely because of the ascent of the sound on which are sung the words "O Martine dulcedo." [5] You may test this more diligently in the Antiphon "Domine qui operati sunt," for if you begin, as many attempt to, on F, in the sixth mode, it will not depart from that mode until the semitone, at "in tabernaculo tuo," on one syllable. But since it is thus in use, and sounds well, it ought not to be emended. Let us inquire, then, whether it does not perhaps begin in another mode, in which all will be found consonant and in which there will be no need for emendation. Begin it, therefore, on G, that is, in the eighth mode, and you will find that it stands regularly in that mode. For this reason, some begin "Domine" as in "Amen dico vobis." [6] From this it is understood that the musician who lightly and presumptuously emends many melodies is ignorant unless he first goes through all the modes to determine whether the melody may perhaps not stand in one or another, nor should he care as much for its similarity to other melodies as for regular truth. But if it suits no mode, let it be emended according to the one with which it least disagrees. This also should be observed: that the emended melody either sound better or depart little from its previous likeness.

[5] St. Martin's Day, Second Vespers, Magnificat Antiphon (*Ant. Vat.*, p. 766). In the Vatican edition the antiphon is given in a shortened form, omitting the passage to which Odo takes exception. But since the "ascent" at "O Martine dulcedo" is repeated at "O sanctissima anima" (retained in the shortened version), the medieval form of the melody need not be quoted here. The "painstaking emendation" of which Odo speaks is made in the Prohemium of his Tonarius, where we read (GS, I, 249a) that the many who take "O beatum pontificem" to be of the second tone are mistaken and that it is properly of the first tone and of the seventh difference. That Odo, in the *Enchiridion*, refers to himself in the third person has led to questions about the authorship of the treatise. It would seem perfectly possible, however, for a writer, particularly in a dialogue, to refer to himself in the third person when speaking of another of his works.

[6] To clarify Odo's comments on this antiphon, the current version of its opening phrase, as given in the *Liber responsorialis* (Solesmes, 1895), p. 382, is compared below with older versions from the monastic antiphoners of Lucca and Worcester (*Paléographie musicale*, Vols. 9 and 12) and with a reconstruction of the "emendation" proposed by Odo. As will be obvious from this comparison, the melody originally involved an E-flat at "in tabernaculo tuo"; this is the "departure" to which Odo objects. Not only has this tone no place in the theoretical system of his time; it also conflicts with his conception of mode in that it gives to the F octave (with b-flat) the internal structure of the G. To avoid these difficulties Lucca and Worcester transpose the melody up a fifth, and Lucca even goes so far as to take the cadence still a step higher; the *Liber responsorialis* simply suppresses the offending accidental. Odo, however, transfers the entire melody to Mode VIII, and to effect this he is obliged to substitute for the original opening, character-

(D) You have warned me well against the error of unskilled singers and have also given me in few words no little knowledge of the careful investigation of the regular monochord, of the verification of regular melodies, and of the emendation of false ones, matters usefully exercising the sense, as is necessary.

7. OF THE LIMITS OF THE MODES

(D) Now tell me of how many sounds a melody ought to be formed.

(M) Some say eight, others nine, others ten.

(D) Why eight?

(M) Because of the greater division, that is, the diapason, or because the citharas of the ancients had eight strings.

(D) Why nine?

(M) Because of the double diapente, which is bounded by nine pitches. For since from Γ to the fourth step, D, is one diapente, and from this same

---

istic of Mode VI (cf., for example, "O admirabile commercium," *Ant. Vat.*, p. 258), a new one in keeping with his new tonality. Hence his reference to "Amen dico vobis," an antiphon of Mode VIII (*Ant. Vat.*, p. 398).

Liber responsorialis

Do-mi-ne, qui o-pe-ra-ti sunt ju-sti-ti-am, ha-bi-ta-bunt in ta-ber-na-cu-lo tu-o,

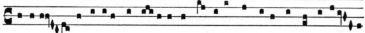

Lucca

Do-mi-ne, qui o-pe-ra-ti sunt ju-sti-ti-am, ha-bi-ta-bunt in ta-ber-na-cu-lo tu-o,

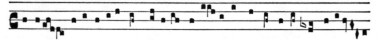

Worcester

Do-mi-ne, qui o-pe-ra-ti sunt ju-sti-ti-am, ha-bi-ta-bunt in ta-ber-na-cu-lo tu-o,

Odo

Do-mi-ne, qui o-pe-ra-ti sunt ju-sti-ti-am, ha-bi-ta-bunt in ta-ber-na-cu-lo tu-o,

fourth step to the eighth, a, is another; from Γ to the eighth step, a, there are nine pitches.

(D) Why ten?

(M) Because of the authority of David's psaltery, or because the triple diatessaron is found at the tenth pitch. For from Γ to the third step, C, is one diatessaron, from the third step, C, to the sixth, F, is a second, from the sixth step, F, to the first ninth, b, is a third; from Γ, therefore, to the first ninth step, b, one counts ten pitches.

(D) May there also be fewer sounds in a melody?

(M) There may indeed be five or four, so situated, however, that the five produce the diapente and the four the diatessaron.

(D) The reasoning you have adduced and the evidence of nearly all melodies proves that what you say is true. Now explain what tone is, that which you more often call mode.

8. WHAT MODE IS, AND WHENCE IT IS DETERMINED OR DISTINGUISHED

(M) A tone, or mode, is a rule which classes every melody according to its final. For unless you know the final you cannot know where the melody ought to begin or how far it ought to ascend and descend.

(D) What rule does the beginning take from the final?

(M) Every beginning ought to concord with its final in one of the be-fore-mentioned six consonances. No sound may begin a melody, except it be the final itself or be consonant with it in some one of these six consonances. And whatever sounds agree with the final by means of these same six consonances may also begin a melody having this final, provided that a melody which ends on the fifth step, E, the first of the semitones in the third mode, is often found to begin on the tenth step, c, removed from the fifth step, E, by a diapente plus semitone.

The distinctions, too, that is, the places at which we repeatedly pause in a melody and at which we divide it, ought obviously to end in each mode with the same sounds with which a melody in that mode may begin. And where each mode best and most often begins, there as a rule it best and most suitably begins and ends its distinctions. Several distinctions ought to end with the sound which concludes the mode, the masters teach, for if more distinctions be made in some other sound than be made in this one, they desire the melody to be ended in that other sound and compel it to be changed from the mode in which it was. A melody, in other words, belongs most to the mode in which the majority of its distinctions lie. For the beginnings, too, are found most often and most suitably on the sound which concludes the melody. You may confirm what has been said by example in the Antiphon "Tribus miraculis": [7] this is one distinction; "ornatum diem sanctum colimus" is a second; "hodie stella Magos duxit ad praesepium" is a third; "hodie vinum ex aqua factum est ad nuptias" is a fourth; "hodie a Joanne Christus baptizari voluit" is the last. And so you see that in a regular melody several distinctions begin and end in the mode and that melodies begin and end on the same sound.

9. OF THE LIMITS OF THE MODES

(D) That these things are as you say is everywhere supported by the authority of singing masters. But proceed; what rule with regard to ascent and descent does a melody take from its final?

(M) In acute or high melodies, as in the first, third, fifth, and seventh modes, no melody ought to ascend further above its final than to the eighth sound, the sound having the same letter as the final, and this because of the special quality of the division which we call diapason: such a melody has below its final one sound. In lower melodies, as in the second, fourth, sixth, and eighth modes, let there be no descent below the final to any sound not joined to it by means of one of the six before-mentioned consonances; in ascent the progression is from the final by means of these same six consonances to the fifth sound, indeed sometimes as far as the sixth. On what sounds the melodies in all the modes most often begin, according to the present use, you will perceive in their formulas.

10. THE EIGHT MODES

(D) Now that you have shown that the melodies in all the modes take a rule from the final, it is time to explain how many modes, or tones, there are.

(M) Some count four modes.

(D) For what reason?

(M) Because every regular melody may end on any one of four of the sounds of the monochord.

(D) Which sounds are these?

(M) The fourth step, D, on which concludes the mode which we call Authentus Protus, that is, the first author or leader; the fifth step, E, on which concludes the mode which we call Authentus Deuterus, that is, the second author or leader; the sixth step, F, on which concludes the Authentus Tritus, that is, the third author or leader; and the seventh step, G, on which concludes the Authentus Tetrardus, that is, the fourth author or leader. These four, moreover, are divided into eight.

---

7 Epiphany, Second Vespers, Magnificat Antiphon (*Ant. Vat.*, p. 272).

(D) For what reason?

(M) For the sake of high and low melodies. For when a melody in the Authentus Protus is acute or high, we call the mode the Authentus Protus. But if in the same Authentus Protus it is grave or low, we call it the Plaga Proti.

(D) Why Plaga Proti?

(M) Plaga Proti, that is, a part of the first, because it ends on the same part, that is, on the same place or step of the monochord on which the Authentus Protus ended, the fourth, D. In a similar way, when a melody in the Authentus Deuterus is acute we call it the Authentus Deuterus, but if it is grave we name it the Plaga Deuteri. In the same manner, we say of the Authentus Tritus, Plaga Triti, and of the Authentus Tetrardus, Plaga Tetrardi. Usage teaches, moreover, to say, instead of Authentus Protus and Plaga Proti, first and second mode; instead of Authentus Deuterus and Plaga Deuteri, third and fourth mode; instead of Authentus Tritus and its Plaga, fifth and sixth mode; instead of Authentus Tetrardus and its Plaga, seventh and eighth mode. There are then eight modes, by means of which every melody, proceeding in different directions, is varied by eight dissimilar qualities.

(D) In what way shall I be able to perceive their differences and common characteristics?

(M) By means of tones and semitones. For where tones and semitones are formed alike, there also the remaining consonances are formed alike. Wherever there are two tones and a semitone, there also will be a diatessaron, and wherever three tones and a semitone are grouped together, there also the diapente will not be wanting. The remaining consonances are to be understood in a similar way.

· · · · ·

(D) Since I have difficulty in finding even a few melodies which violate these rules, I have no doubt that their scarcity and, so to speak, furtive singularity are the work of presumptuous and corrupt singers.

(M) A rule, certainly, is a general mandate of any art; thus things which are singular do not obey the rules of art.

(D) But add, I pray you, according to the position of each sound, a few things more about the law of the modes.

(M) Your request deserves an answer. For each sound bears a resemblance to some one of the aforesaid modes.

For example, Γ, since it has above it two tones, adding after these a semitone and two tones and then a semitone and a tone, rightly bears a similarity to the seventh mode, for the final of the seventh mode also sounds the diapason to Γ. Likewise the first step, A, since it has below it a tone, but above it a tone, a semitone, and two tones, observes the rule of the first mode and is hence not without reason called first. But the second step, B, since one descends below it by two tones and ascends above it by a semitone and two tones, obeys the usual rule of the fourth mode. In addition, the third step, C, since it has below it a semitone and two tones, but above it two tones and a semitone and then three tones, is upheld by the property of the fifth or sixth mode.

Now, however, the eighth step, a, occupies the first place in similarity to the first step, whose diapason it is. On the other hand, if you consider it in connection with the first ninth step, b, it will have in descent a tone, but in ascent a semitone and three tones, like the third mode. The first ninth step, b, comprises in descent a semitone and two tones, like the sixth mode, but in ascent—either because three tones follow, or rather because it is not joined by any affinity to the following diatessaron—it has no regular resemblance to any mode and indeed cannot be formed by a diapason from the foregoing; consequently you will find that neither a melody nor a distinction may begin or end with it, except by a fault. The second ninth step, ♮, like the second step, B, resembles the fourth mode. The tenth step, c, like the third step, C, agrees with the fifth or sixth mode. But if it be deprived of the second ninth step, ♮, it will, in a different fashion, have below it a tone, a semitone, and two tones, but above it two tones and a semitone, on the analogy of the eighth mode, from whose final it marks a diatessaron.

The remaining sounds, which follow, are because of the similarity of their letters easily dealt with, as this diagram shows:

							III							
VII	I		V	I	III	V	VII	I		V	I	III	V	VII	I
Γ	A	B	C	D	E	F	G	a	♮	c	d	e	f	g	a / a
VIII	II	IV	VI	II	IV	VI	VIII	II	IV	VI	II	IV	VI	VIII	II
							VIII							

From what has been said, the diligent inquirer will, with the aid of Divine Grace, understand many other matters both concerning the modes and concerning the remaining rules of this art. But if he is negligent, or if he should presumptuously think to comprehend them by the keenness of his wit and not by Divine enlightenment, either he will comprehend them not at all or, so long as he does not return thanks to the Giver, he will become (God forbid!) the vassal of his pride and the less loyal to his Creator, who is blessed, world without end. Amen.

15. Guido of Arezzo

A Benedictine monk who made important contributions to the development of musical theory in the Middle Ages, Guido was probably born near Paris about 995 and received his education in the Benedictine abbey of St. Maur-des-Fossés. From there he went first to the abbey of Pomposa in northern Italy, and later to Arezzo. His reputation as a scholar in the field of musical theory brought Guido to Rome, where he convinced Pope John XIX of the excellence of the improvements that he had introduced into the teaching of music and singing. Guido became prior of the monastery at Avellano in 1029 and died about 1050.

Prologus antiphonarii sui [1]

[ca. 1025]

IN OUR TIMES, of all men, singers are the most foolish. For in any art those things which we know of ourselves are much more numerous than those which we learn from a master. As soon as they have read the Psalter attentively, small boys know the meanings of all books. Rustics understand the science of agriculture at once, for he who knows how to prune one vineyard, to plant one tree, to load one ass, does not hesitate to do in all cases as he did in the one, if not even better. But marvelous singers, and singers' pupils, though they sing every day for a hundred years, will never sing one antiphon, not even a short one, of themselves, without a master, losing time enough in singing to have learned thoroughly both sacred and secular letters.

And what is the most dangerous thing of all, many clerics and monks of the religious order neglect the psalms, the sacred readings, the nocturnal vigils, and the other works of piety that arouse and lead us on to

1 Text: Gerbert, *Scriptores*, II, 34–37.

everlasting glory, while they apply themselves with unceasing and most foolish effort to the science of singing which they can never master.

Who does not also bewail this (which is at once a grave error and a dangerous discord in Holy Church), that when we celebrate the divine office we are often seen rather to strive among ourselves than to praise God, in short, that scarcely one agrees with another, neither the pupil with his master, nor the pupil with his fellow pupils? It is for this reason that the antiphoners are not one, nor yet a few, but rather as many as are the masters in the single churches; and that the antiphoner is now commonly said to be, not Gregory's, but Leo's, or Albert's, or someone's else. And since to learn one is most difficult, there can be no doubt that to learn many is impossible.

In which matter, since the masters change many things arbitrarily, little or no blame should attach to me if I depart from common use in scarcely more than a few respects in order that every chant may return uniformly to a common rule of art. And inasmuch as all these evils and many others have arisen from the fault of those who make antiphoners, I strongly urge and maintain that no one should henceforth presume to provide an antiphoner with neumes except he understand this business and know how to do it properly according to the rules here laid down. Otherwise, without having first been a disciple of truth, he will most certainly be a master of error.

It is in this way, then, that I have decided, with God's help, to write this antiphoner so that hereafter, by means of it, any intelligent and studious person may learn singing and so that, after he has thoroughly learned a part of it through a master, he will unhesitatingly understand the rest of it by himself without one. As to this, should anyone doubt that I am telling the truth, let him come, make a trial, and see what small boys can do under our direction, boys who until now have been beaten for their gross ignorance of the psalms and vulgar letters, who often do not know how to pronounce the words and syllables of the very antiphon which, without a master, they sing correctly by themselves, something which, with God's help, any intelligent and studious person will be able to do if he try to understand the intention with which we have arranged the neumes.

The sounds, then, are so arranged that each sound, however often it may be repeated in a melody, is found always in its own row. And in order that you may better distinguish these rows, lines are drawn close together, and some rows of sounds occur on the lines themselves, others in the intervening intervals or spaces. Then the sounds on one line or in one space all sound alike. And in order that you may also understand to which lines or spaces each sound belongs, certain letters of the monochord are written at the beginning of the lines or spaces and the lines are also gone over in colors, thereby indicating that in the whole antiphoner and in every melody those lines or spaces which have one and the same letter or color, however many they may be, sound alike throughout, as though all were on one line. For just as the line indicates complete identity of sounds, so the letter or color indicates complete identity of lines, and hence of sounds also.

Then if you find the second row of sounds everywhere distinguished by such a letter or colored line, you will also know readily that this same identity of sounds and neumes runs through all the second rows. Understand the same of the third, fourth, and remaining rows, whether you count up or down. It is then most certainly true that all neumes or sounds similarly or dissimilarly formed on lines of the same letter or color sound alike throughout, the line being lettered or colored in the same way, and that on different lines or in different spaces even similarly formed neumes sound by no means alike. Hence, be the formation of the neumes as perfect as you please, without the addition of letters or colors it is altogether meaningless and worthless.

For we use two colors, namely yellow and red, and by means of them I teach you a rule that will enable you to know readily to what tone and to what letter of the monochord every neume and any sound belong, most useful if, as is very convenient, you make frequent use of the monochord and of the formulas of the tones.[2]

Now, as I shall show fully later on, the letters of the monochord are seven. Wherever, then, you see the color yellow, there is the third letter, C, and wherever you see the color red, there is the sixth letter, F, whether these colors be on the lines or between them. Hence in the third row beneath the yellow is the first letter, A, belonging to the first and second tone; above this, next to the yellow, is the second letter, B, belonging to the third and fourth tone; then, on the yellow itself, is the third letter or sound, C, belonging to the fifth and sixth tone; immediately above the yellow and third below the red is the fourth letter, D, belonging to the first and second tone; nearest the red is the fifth letter, E, belonging to the third and fourth tone; on the red itself is the sixth letter, F, belonging to the fifth and sixth tone; next above the red is the seventh letter, G, belonging to the seventh and eighth tone; then, in the third row above the

2 For the formulas of the tones see p. 104 above, note 2.

red, below the yellow, is repeated the first letter, a, belonging, as already explained, to the first and second tone; after this, differing in no respect from the
foregoing, are repeated all the rest; all which things this diagram [3] will teach
you quite clearly.

```
VII  I  III V  I  III V  VII I  III V  I  III V  VII I  III V  I
                                                  a  ♮   c   d
Γ    A  B  C   D  E  F  G   a  ♮  c   d  e  f   g   a  ♮   c   d
VIII II IV VI  II IV VI VIII II IV VI  II IV VI VIII II  IV  VI  II
```

Although each letter or sound belongs always to two tones, the formulas of the second, fourth, six, and eighth tones agree much better and more
frequently in the single neumes or sounds, for the formulas of the first,
third, fifth, and seventh agree only when the melody, descending from
above, concludes with a low note.[4]

Know, finally, that if you would make progress with these notes, you
must learn by heart a fair number of melodies so that through these single
neumes, modes, or sounds you may acquire through memory an understanding of all, of whatever sort they may be. For it is indeed quite another thing to know something by heart than it is to sing something by
heart, since only the wise can do the former while persons without fore-
sight can often do the latter. As to the simple understanding of neumes,
let these things suffice.

How sounds are liquescent; whether they should be sung as connected
or as separate; which ones are retarded and tremulous, and which has-
tened; how a chant is divided by distinctions; whether the following or
preceding sound be higher, lower, or equal sounding; by a simple discussion all this is shown in the shape of the neumes itself, if the neumes
are, as they should be, carefully put together.

---

3 Guido's diagram should be compared with
Odo's (p. 116 above).

4 To put it differently, the final will as a rule
occur more frequently in plagal melodies than
in authentic ones. Thus the correspondence of a
given step to the appropriate plagal formula will
be greater than to the authentic formula with
which it is paired.

16. Guido of Arezzo

Epistola de ignoto cantu [1]

[ca. 1030]

To the most blessed and beloved Brother Michael, Guido, by many vicissitudes cast down and strengthened:

Either the times are hard or the judgments of the Divine ordinance are obscure when truth is trampled upon by falsehood and love is trampled upon by envy, which rarely ceases to accompany our order; by this means, the conspiring of the Philistines punishes the Israelitish transgression, lest if anything should promptly turn out according to our wishes, the mortal soul should perish in its self-confidence. For our actions are good only when we ascribe to the Creator all that we are able to accomplish.

Hence it is that you see me banished from pleasant domains and yourself suffocated so that you can scarcely breathe. In which plight I say that we are much like a certain artisan who presented to Augustus Caesar an incomparable treasure, namely, flexible glass. Thinking that because he could do something beyond the power of all others, he deserved a reward beyond all others, he was by the worst of fortunes sentenced to death, lest, if glass could be made as durable as it is marvelous, the entire royal treasure, consisting of various metals, should suddenly become worthless. And so from that time on, accursed envy has deprived mortals of this boon, as it once deprived them of Eden. For since the artisan's envy was unwilling to teach anyone his secret, the king's envy could destroy the artisan along with his art. [2]

For which reason, moved by a divinely inspired charity, I have brought to you and to as many others as I have been able a grace divinely bestowed on me, the most unworthy of men; namely, that those who come after

---

1 Text: Gerbert, *Scriptores*, II, 43–46, 50.
2 Cf. Petronius, *Satires*. 51; there are variants of the story in Pliny, *Naturalis historia*, xxxvi, 26, and Dio Cassius, *Roman History*, lvii, 21.

us, when they learn with the greatest ease the ecclesiastical melodies which I and all my predecessors learned only with the greatest difficulty, they will desire for me and for you and my other helpers eternal salvation, and by the mercy of God our sins will be remitted, or at least from the gratitude of so many will come some prayer for our souls.

For if at present those who have succeeded in gaining only an imperfect knowledge of singing in ten years of study intercede most devoutly before God for their teachers, what think you will be done for us and our helpers, who can produce a perfect singer in the space of one year, or at the most in two? Even if the customary baseness of mankind should prove ungrateful for such benefits, will not a just God reward our labors? Or, since this is God's work and we can do nothing without Him, shall we have no reward? Forbid the thought. For even the Apostle, though whatever is done is done by God's grace, sings none the less: "I have fought a good fight, I have finished my course, I have kept the faith. Henceforth there is laid up for me a crown of righteousness." [3]

Confident therefore in our hope of reward, we set about a task of such usefulness, and since after many storms the long-desired fair weather has returned, we must felicitously set sail.

But since you in your captivity are distrustful of liberty, I will set forth the situation in full. John, holder of the most high apostolic seat, who now governs the Roman Church,[4] hearing of the fame of our school and greatly wondering how, by means of our Antiphoner, boys could know songs which they had never heard, invited me through three emissaries to come to him. I therefore went to Rome with Dom Grunwald, the most reverend Abbot, and Dom Peter, Provost of the canons of the church of Arezzo, by the standards of our time a most learned man. The Pope, accordingly, was greatly pleased by my arrival, conversing much with me and inquiring of many matters. After repeatedly looking through our Antiphoner as if it were some prodigy, and reflecting on the rules prefixed to it, he did not dismiss the subject or leave the place where he sat until he had satisfied his desire by himself learning to sing a verse without hearing it beforehand, thus quickly finding true in his own case what he could hardly believe of others.

What need I say more? I was prevented by illness from remaining in Rome even a short time longer, as the summer heat in places swampy and near the sea was threatening our destruction. We finally came to the agreement that I should return later, at the beginning of winter, at which time

---

[3] II Timothy 4:7–8.   [4] John XIX, pope from 1024 to 1033.

I should reveal this work of mine more fully to the Pope and his clerk, who had enjoyed the foretaste of it.

A few days after this, desiring to see your spiritual father Dom Guido, Abbot of Pomposa, a man highly endeared to God and men by the merit of his virtue and wisdom, and a beloved friend, I paid him a visit. When he with his clear intelligence saw our Antiphoner, he at once recognized its value and had faith in it. He regretted that he had once given countenance to our rivals and asked me to come to Pomposa, urging upon me that monasteries were to be preferred to bishops' residences, especially Pomposa, because of its zeal for learning, which now by the grace of God and the industry of the most reverend Guido ranks foremost in Italy.

Swayed by the prayers of so eminent a father, and obeying his instructions, I wish first, God helping me, to confer distinction upon so notable a monastery by this work and further to reveal myself to the monks as a monk. Since nearly all the bishops have been convicted of simony, I should fear to enter into relations with any of their number.

As I cannot come to you at present, I am in the meantime addressing to you a most excellent method of finding an unknown melody, recently given to us by God and found most useful in practice. Further, I most reverently salute Dom Martin, the Prior of the Holy Congregation, our greatest helper, and with the most earnest entreaties commend my miserable self to his prayers, and I admonish Brother Peter, who, nourished by our milk, now feeds on the rudest barley, and after golden bowls of wine, drinks a mixture of vinegar, to remember one who remembers him.

. . . . .

To find an unknown melody, most blessed brother, the first and common procedure is this. You sound on the monochord the letters belonging to each neume, and by listening you will be able to learn the melody as if from hearing it sung by a teacher. But this procedure is childish, good indeed for beginners, but very bad for pupils who have made some progress. For I have seen many keen-witted philosophers who had sought out not merely Italian, but French, German, and even Greek teachers for the study of this art, but who, because they relied on this procedure alone, could never become, I will not say skilled musicians, but even choristers, nor could they duplicate the performance of our choir boys.

We do not need to have constant recourse to the voice of a singer or to the sound of some instrument to become acquainted with an unknown melody, so that as if blind we should seem never to go forward without a leader; we need to implant the differences and qualities of the individual sounds and of all descents and ascents deep in the memory. You will then have a most easy and approved method of finding an unknown melody, provided there is someone present to teach the pupil, not merely from a written textbook, but rather by informal discussion, according to our practice. For after I began teaching this procedure to boys, some of them were able to sing an unknown melody before the third day, which by other methods would not have been possible in many weeks.

If, therefore, you wish to commit any note or neume to memory so that it will promptly recur to you, whenever you wish, in any melody whatever, known or unknown to you, and so that you will be able to sound it at once and with full confidence, you must mark that note or neume at the beginning of some especially familiar melody; and to retain each and every note in your memory, you must have at ready command a melody of this description which begins with that note. For example, let it be this melody, which, in teaching boys, I use at the beginning and even to the very end:

C   D   F   DE D   D   D   C   D E   E
Ut que-ant la - xis   re - so - na - re fi - bris

EFG E   D   EC D   F   G   aG   FED D
Mi- ra ge-sto - rum   fa - mu - li tu - o-   rum,

GaG FE F   G D   a   G   aF   Ga a
Sol - ve pol - lu-ti   la - bi - i re - a - tum,

GF   ED C   E   D
San - cte Jo - an - nes.

Do you not see how, in this melody, the six phrases begin each with a different note? If, trained as I have described, you know the beginning of each phrase so that you can at once and confidently begin any one you wish, you will be able to sing these notes in their proper qualities whenever you see them. Then, when you hear any neume that has not been written down, consider carefully which of these phrases is best adapted to the last note of the neume, so that this last note and the first note of your phrase are of the same pitch. And be sure that the neume ends on the note with which the phrase corresponding to it begins. And when you begin to sing an unknown melody that has been written down, take great care to end each neume so correctly that its last note joins well with the beginning of the phrase which begins with the note on which the neume ends. To sing an unknown melody competently as soon as you see it written down, or, hearing an unwritten melody, to see quickly how to write it down well, this rule will be of the greatest use to you.

I afterwards adapted short fragments of melody to the single sounds in order.[5] Closely examining the phrases of these, you will rejoice to find at the beginnings of the phrases all the ascending and descending progressions of each note in turn. If you succeed in singing at will the phrases of each and every one of these fragments, you will have learned, by a rule most brief and easy, the exceedingly difficult and manifold varieties of all the neumes. All these matters, which we can hardly indicate in any way with letters, we can easily lay bare by a simple discussion.

. . . .

The few words on the form of the modes and neumes which I have set down, both in prose and in verse, as a prologue to the Antiphoner [6] will perhaps briefly and sufficiently open the portals of the art of music. And let the painstaking seek out our little book called *Micrologus* [7] and also read the book *Enchiridion*,[8] most lucidly composed by the most reverend Abbot Odo, from whose example I have departed only in the forms of the notes, since I have simplified my treatment for the sake of the young, in this not following Boethius, whose treatise is useful to philosophers, but not to singers.

---

5 These "short fragments of melody" (*brevissimae symphoniae*) seem not to have been preserved.

6 In prose, pp. 117–120, in verse, GS, II, 25–34.

7 GS, II, 2–24, or edited by A. M. Amelli

(1904). There are German translations by Raimund Schlecht in *Monatshefte für Musik-Geschichte*, V (1873), no. 9–11, and by Michael Hermesdorff (1876).

8 Pages 103–116.

17. From the Scholia enchiriadis

The polyphonic practice of the ninth and tenth centuries is known to us, not through practical monuments, but through theoretical writings which give rules for the improvisation of a simple counterpoint to a given plainsong. The earliest of these writings are the ninth-century *Musica enchiriadis*, its contemporary *Scholia*, or commentary, extracts from which are translated below, and the related "Cologne treatise" and "Paris treatise"; formerly ascribed to Hucbald of St. Amand (died 930), more recently to Otger, abbot of St. Pons de Tomieres (died 940), or to Hoger, abbot of Werden (died 902), they are now perhaps best left anonymous. The view of music set forth in this group of writings embraces a number of elements borrowed from Graeco-Roman authors, among them the concept of music as a branch of mathematics, the acceptance of Pythagorean number-theory and the Pythagorean division of the monochord, the rejection of "imperfect" consonance, the theoretical construction of a "system" from similar tetrachords, modeled on the "complete system" of ancient Greek music, and the use of a sign-notation based upon a misunderstanding of the notations of ancient Greek music (the so-called "Daseia" notation).

Of Symphonies [1]

[ca. 900]

(Disciple) What is a symphony?

(Master) A sweet blending of certain sounds, three of which are simple—diapason, diapente, and diatessaron—and three composite—double diapason, diapason plus diapente, and diapason plus diatessaron.

(D) Which is the symphony of the diapason?

1 Text: Gerbert, *Scriptores*, I, 184–196. There is a German translation by Schlecht in *Monatshefte für Musik-Geschichte*, VI–VII (1874–75).

(M) That which is sung at the octave, six pitches intervening.

(D) Which is the diapente and which the diatessaron?

(M) The diapente occurs at the fifth, the diatessaron at the fourth, just as in pentachords and tetrachords the extremes agree with one another.

(D) Why is the diapason so called?

(M) Because the ancient cithara had only eight strings, the Greek word "diapason" being translated by the Latin "ex omnibus." [2]

(D) Why are the diapente and the diatessaron so called?

(M) The diapente is called "from five" because it contains five pitches; the diatessaron includes four pitches, being translated "from four."

(D) How is the diapason sung?

(M) Whenever in descending or ascending we pass from one sound to another in such a way that the higher and lower sounds are not so much consonant as equal-sounding, being by this agreement concordant, these sounds combine in the diapason; as when we descend from H to A or ascend from H to P, following the diagram given below.

A B C D E F G H I K L M N O P

| Relaxed | | Intense | |
| diapason | | diapason | |

For whether we take the one after the other at the octave, or whether we sing two in one with two sounds that are equal-sounding, we form the harmony of the simple diapason. And if we sing three in one with three such sounds we form the harmony of the double diapason. Furthermore, if we sing at the fifteenth, leaving out the inner sound, we shall also have the double diapason.

Let us sing them all in the way I have described. [8]

OF THE DIAPASON AND DOUBLE DIAPASON

This symphony, since it is easier and more open, is called greatest and first.

Nos qui vivimus, benedicimus Domino, ex hoc nunc et us-que in sae-cu-lum

2 Cf. Cassiodorus, *Institutiones*, II, v, § 7 (p. 89 above).

8 The given melody used in the examples which follow is the psalmody of the Tonus Peregrinus

OF THE DIAPENTE

The symphony of the diapente follows. This is formed whenever at the level of the fifth we take the one after the other or lead both in one in the way indicated below.

In this way the diapente is sung simply. The first composite symphony of the diapente is formed when the organal voice is doubled at the diapason so that the principal voice becomes a mean, as the fifth between prime and octave. I call principal the voice presenting the melody; organal, on the other hand, the one added below it for the sake of the symphony. Let us sing this in the way indicated below.

The second composite symphony of the diapente is formed when the voice which we have called principal is doubled at the diapason so that the organal voice becomes a mean, as the octave between fifth and twelfth.[4] Let us sing it in the way indicated below.

Nos qui vivimus, benedicimus Domino, ex hoc nunc et us-que in sae-cu-lum.

(or Tonus novissimus, as it is called by the author of the *Commemoratio brevis*, GS, I, 218). Although in the original notation the question is left open, we have assumed that the second tone of the given melody is to be understood as b-flat (not b-natural) and that a corresponding modification is to be made in the organum when it is at the fifth. Only on this basis do the examples

illustrating the organum at the fourth become intelligible. For a discussion of the melody of the Tonus Peregrinus, as given in the *Scholia enchiriadis* and *Commemoratio brevis*, see Dom Paolo Ferretti, *Estetica gregoriana*, I (Rome, 1934), 339, 355–363.

4 For *inter quartam ac undecimam* read *inter quintam ac duodecimam;* cf. p. 132 below.

The third composite symphony of the diapente is formed when the organal voice is doubled below at the diapason so that the principal voice is the highest, as the twelfth above octave and prime. This consonance at the twelfth is also concordant, the inner voice being left out.

The fourth composite symphony of the diapente is formed when the principal voice is doubled above at the diapason so that the organal voice is the lowest, as the prime below fifth and twelfth. This is concordant in a similar way, the inner voice being again left out.

The fifth composite symphony of the diapente is sung by a fourfold diversity of voices when both voices have been doubled at the diapason, as when to the fifth and twelfth the prime and octave supply the organum.

Let all be sung in the way indicated below.

The sixth composite symphony of the diapente occurs when the organal voice is the highest, as the fifteenth above twelfth and fifth in the way indicated below.

Numerous further species of this same symphony can also be produced if either or both voices be tripled at the double diapason.

OF THE DIATESSARON

The symphony of the diatessaron follows. This occurs when at the level of the fourth we sing in one. Be it known, however, that this is not effected

where it is explained that in the second composite symphony of the diapente the principle voice stands a fourth below and a fifth above the inner organal voice. We have altered Gerbert's musical example to agree with the emended text.

as simply as at the other larger intervals, the organum being derived by a certain natural law about which we shall speak later. Nevertheless, if it be performed with the modest retardation most suitable to it and attended with proper diligence, there will be a most admirable smoothness of harmony.

The composite symphonies of the diatessaron are made in the same ways as were those of the diapente. For the first composite symphony of the diatessaron occurs when the organal voice is doubled at the diapason so that the principal voice becomes a mean, as the fourth between prime and octave in the way indicated below.

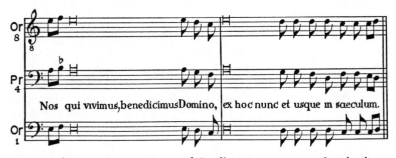

A second composite symphony of the diatessaron occurs when in the opposite way the principal voice is doubled at the diapason so that the organal voice becomes a mean, as the octave between fourth and eleventh.

The third composite symphony of the diatessaron occurs when the organal voice is doubled below at the diapason so that the principal voice becomes the highest, as the eleventh above octave and prime.

The fourth composite symphony of the diatessaron occurs when the principal voice is doubled above at the diapason so that the organal voice becomes the lowest, as the prime below fourth and eleventh.

The fifth composite symphony of the diatessaron occurs when both voices, namely principal and organal, are doubled at the diapason so that to the fourth and eleventh the prime and octave supply the organum.

The sixth composite symphony of the diatessaron occurs when the organal voice is the highest, as the fifteenth above eleventh and fourth. Let it be sung in the way indicated below.

And be it noted that whether the principal voice or the organal voice or both voices be doubled at the diapason the place of the highest voice can always be supplied by the voice of boys.

(D) What difference is there, I ask, between the first composite symphony of the diapente and the second of the diatessaron, when both here and there the extreme voices are separated from the inner voice by the same intervals? And similarly, what difference is there between the second composite symphony of the diapente and the first of the diatessaron?

(M) If you inquire why in the first composite symphony of the diapente the inner voice is principal rather than organal, while in the second
composite symphony of the diatessaron the inner voice is organal rather
than principal, when both here and there the inner voice is related to the
extreme voices by the same intervals; and, on the other hand, why in the
second composite symphony of the diapente the inner voice is called organal, while in the first composite symphony of the diatessaron it is
principal; know that the reason is this: in the symphony of the diatessaron
the organal voice does not accompany the principal voice so simply and
absolutely as in that of the diapente, for by a certain natural law of its
own it stands still in certain places and is unable to proceed further consonantly, just as in the diagrams already given it was shown how it does
not descend below the fourth sound of the tetrachord.

Be it known, moreover, that in the composite symphonies already mentioned the diatessaron and diapente differ also by a certain other propriety.
For since there is always a reversion of the tropes or tones at the fifth and
octave, and in the symphony of the diapente, since at the fifth the lower
voice responds to the upper with the same variety of trope, we must respond to either voice from its octave with the same trope.

Thus it follows that, when the organal voice has been doubled at the
diapason, making the principal voice a mean, the organal voice is separated
from the inner voice below by fifths and above by fourths, this being the
first composite symphony of the diapente; moreover, when the principal
voice has been doubled at the diapason, making the organal voice a mean,
the principal voice is distinguished from the inner voice below by fourths
and above by fifths, this being the second composite symphony of the
diapente.

In the opposite way, in the symphony of the diatessaron, since at the
fourth the lower voice does not respond to the upper with the same trope,
we must respond to the principal and organal voices from their octaves,
not with the same trope, but to each with its own.

Thus it follows that, when the organal voice has been doubled at the
diapason, making the principal voice a mean, the organal voice is distant
from the inner voice below by fourths and above by fifths, this being the
first composite symphony of the diatessaron; moreover, when the principal voice has been doubled at the diapason, making the organal voice a
mean, the principal voice is disjoined from the inner voice below by fifths
and above by fourths, this being the second composite symphony of the
diatessaron.

All of these are shown in the diagrams already given.

Have you a further question? [5]

(D) Inasmuch as you have said that in the symphony of the diapente the tropes sounded together are the same, while in the symphony of the diatessaron they are not, and that for this reason, in the already mentioned composite symphonies of both consonances, the inner voice, although separated from the extreme voices by the same intervals, is here principal but there organal, since the same trope does not occur both here and there; I ask what the difference is between the principal and organal voices in the symphony of the diapente, where the tropes are not dissimilar.

(M) Recall now what was said: in the symphony of the diapente, when the organal voice has been doubled at the diapason, if the inner voice were related to the extreme voices by the same interval, no difference between the principal and organal voices would be apparent. Now, however, since the organal voice stands below the principal voice at the fifth, but through the diapason above it at the fourth (just as vice versa in the symphony of the diatessaron the organal voice stands below the principal voice at the fourth, but through the diapason above it at the fifth), and since, when the principal voice has been doubled at the diapason, the situation is similar; since the inner voice is not related to the extreme voices by the same intervals, you can readily understand how the virtue of the symphony of the diapason, which multiplies both voices, also determines which voices are principal and which organal.

(D) Why cannot the organal voice in the symphony of the diatessaron agree with the principal voice so absolutely as is the case with the other symphonies?

(M) Since, as was said, the same tropes do not recur at the level of the fourth and the modes of different tropes cannot be maintained throughout or at the same time, for this reason in the symphony of the diatessaron the principal and organal voices do not agree throughout at the level of the fourth.

(D) I wish also to know how at the fourth the genus of the tropes is dissimilar.

(M) This you will easily perceive. For whether we transpose it one tone higher or to the fourth below, the mode of different tropes may be discerned by the attentive ear. Sing in the way indicated below:

a	♮	c	d	c	♮	a
G	a	♮	c	♮	a	G
F	G	a	♮	a	G	F
E	F	G	a	G	F	E

5 Gerbert's assignment of this question to the disciple is emended by Schlecht.

(D) I discern plainly that by this transposition the authentic tone Protus passes over into the authentic Deuterus. But will you give now the reason why at some levels sounds are thus consonant, while at others they are either discrepant or not so much in agreement?

(M) Certainly one is at liberty to consider what reasons God has assigned, and thus in a delightful way we perceive a little the causes of the agreement and discrepancy of sounds, as well as the nature of the different tropes and why in transposing they pass over into other species or revert again to their own. For just as in counting absolutely the numerical series used (that is, 1, 2, 3, 4, and so forth) is simple and by reason of its simplicity easily grasped, even by boys, but when one thing is compared unequally with another it falls under various species of inequality; so in Music, the daughter of Arithmetic (that is, the science of number), sounds are enumerated by a simple order, but when sounded in relation to others they yield not only the various species of the delightful harmonies, but also the most delightful reasons for them.

(D) How is Harmony born of Arithmetic as from a mother; and what is Harmony, and what Music?

(M) Harmony we consider a concordant blending of unequal sounds. Music is the theory of concord itself. And as it is joined throughout to the theory of numbers, as are also the other disciplines of Mathematics, so it is through numbers that we must understand it.

(D) What are the disciplines of Mathematics?

(M) Arithmetic, Geometry, Music, and Astronomy.

(D) What is Mathematics?

(M) Doctrinal science.

(D) Why doctrinal?

(M) Because it considers abstract quantities.

(D) What are abstract quantities?

(M) Those which being without material, that is, without corporeal admixture, are treated by the intellect alone. In quantities, moreover, multitudes, magnitudes, their opposites, forms, equalities, relationships, and many other things which, to speak with Boethius,[6] are by nature incorporeal and immutable, prevailing by reason, are changed by the participation of the corporeal and through the operation of variable matter become mutable and inconstant. These quantities, further, are variously considered in Arithmetic, in Music, in Geometry, and in Astronomy. For these four disciplines are not arts of human invention, but considerable

---

6 This discussion of the quadrivium leans heavily on Cassiodorus, *Institutiones*, II, iii, § 21 (cf.   p. 88, note 6) and Boethius, *De institutione arithmetica*, I, i.

investigations of divine works; and by most marvelous reasons they lead ingenious minds to understand the creatures of the world; so that those who through these things know God and His eternal divinity are inexcusable if they do not glorify Him and give thanks.

(D) What is Arithmetic?

(M) The discipline of numerable quantities in themselves.

(D) What is Music?

(M) The rational discipline of agreement and discrepancy in sounds according to numbers in their relation to those things which are found in sounds.[7]

(D) What is Geometry?

(M) The discipline of immobile magnitude and of forms.

(D) What is Astronomy?

(M) The discipline of mobile magnitude which contemplates the course of the heavenly bodies and all figures and considers with inquiring reason the orbits of the stars about themselves and about the earth.

(D) How is it that through numerable science the three other disciplines exist?

(M) Because everything comprehended by these disciplines exists through reason formed of numbers and without numbers can be neither understood nor made known. For how can we learn what a triangle or quadrangle is, and the other concerns of Geometry, unless we already know what three and four are?

(D) In no way.

(M) Of what use is it in Astronomy to know the theory without knowing number? Whence do we know the risings and settings, the slowness and velocity of the wandering stars? Whence do we perceive the phases of the moon with its manifold variations, or what part of the zodiac is occupied by the sun or moon or any other planet you will? Is it not that as all things are set in motion by certain laws of number, without number they remain unknown?

(D) It is indeed.

(M) Why is it that, in Music, sounds are equal-sounding at the octave and consonant at the fourth and fifth? And why do they respond as equal-sounding at the fifteenth, as consonant at the twelfth and eleventh? What, moreover, are those measures which join sounds to other sounds so aptly that, if one be a little higher or lower than another, it cannot be concordant with it?

(D) It is surely marvelous that there be these commensurabilities in

---

[7] Cf. Cassiodorus, *Institutiones*, II, iii, § 21 (p. 88).

sounds by which the symphonies agree together so delightfully and the remaining sounds are joined together in order so appropriately. But it is for you to expound those things which you have proposed.

(M) I say that there is equal sound at the octave or diapason because sounds are here brought together by duple relationship (as 6 to 12, or 12 to 24). Similarly, there is equal sound at the fifteenth or double diapason because this symphony is in quadruple proportion (as 6 to 24). At the fifth or diapente, sounds respond consonantly to one another because they are in sesquialtera ratio, the lesser number containing two parts, the greater three (as 6 to 9, or 8 to 12). At the fourth or diatessaron, sounds are consonant because they are in epitrita or sesquitertia ratio, the lesser number containing three parts, the greater four (as 6 to 8, or 9 to 12). Brought together at the twelfth, they are concordant because the diapente responds to the diapason, or sesquialtera to duple (as 18 to 12 and 6, or 8 to 12 and 24), or because the twelfth is in triple proportion (as 18 to 6, or 24 to 8). At the eleventh, they are also consonant because the diatessaron responds to the diapason, or epitrita to duple (as 16 to 12 and 6, or 9 to 12 and 24). And because the diatessaron and the diapente are mutually related, the diatessaron including four sounds, the diapente five, sounds representing the difference between these symphonies are likewise concordant by this relationship, namely by the relationship of epogdous or sesquioctava, the difference between sesquialtera and sesquitertia being always epogdous (in which proportion are 8 and 9, making 16 and 18, making 32 and 36, and so on to infinity).

A diagram of what has been said.

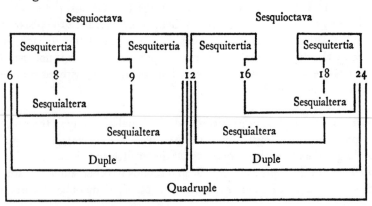

Aside from this, the symphonies of the diapason and double diapason are more perfect than those of the diatessaron and diapente because the former are of multiple inequality, the latter of superparticular, multiple inequality being more perfect than superparticular. Moreover, the sounds of these proportions, that is, of duple, triple, quadruple, sesquialtera, sesquitertia, and sesquioctava, doubtless form consonances or equal sounds because in all the disciplines they are the only commensurate and connumerate relative numbers. It is also on this account that they are assigned to the symphonies and other musical sounds, or rather, that by them the modulated sounds are created. Do you perceive now that Music can be explained only by arithmetical ratios?

(D) I perceive clearly that Arithmetic is necessary to an understanding of Music.

(M) Absolutely necessary, for Music is fashioned wholly in the likeness of numbers. Indeed, if you make one string or pipe twice as long as another of equal thickness (as 12 to 6, or 24 to 12), they will together sound the diapason. If you make another string or pipe of equal diameter longer by a third part of the smaller (as 8 to 6, or 16 to 12) or shorter by a fourth part of the larger (as 9 to 12 or 18 to 24), you will have the consonance of the diatessaron (8 to 6, or 16 to 12, and similarly 9 to 12, or 18 to 24). With 9 to 6, however, or 8 to 12, and similarly with 18 to 12, or 16 to 24, you will have the diapente. Thus it happens that, just as duple contains sesquialtera and sesquitertia (6 and 12, or 12 and 24 containing 8 and 9, or 16 and 18), namely, in an alternate way, so that the number in sesquialtera proportion to the smaller (as 9 to 6, or 18 to 12) is in sub-sesquitertia proportion to the larger (as 9 to 12, or 18 to 24) and on the other hand so that the number in sesquitertia proportion to the smaller (as 8 to 6, or 16 to 12) is in sub-sesquialtera proportion to the larger (as 8 to 12, or 16 to 24); so between two sounds sounding together the diapason, symphonies are always naturally disposed at the fourth and fifth, what is on the one side at the fourth being the diatessaron, what is on the other side at the fifth being the diapente, what there at the fourth sounds the diatessaron sounding here the diapente. Furthermore, just as in sesquioctava proportion 9 exceeds 8, as 18 does 16, and 36 does 32, so if the greater pipe or fiddle-string exceed the smaller by an eighth part, they will together sound the tone.

Whatever is delightful in song is brought about by number through the proportioned dimensions of sounds; whatever is excellent in rhythms, or in songs, or in any rhythmic movements you will, is effected wholly by number. Sounds pass quickly away, but numbers, which are obscured by the corporeal element in sounds and movements, remain. As St. Augustine says: [8]

---

8 *De ordine*, II, xiv–xv; see also his *De libero arbitrio*, II, xvi, translated into English by Rich- ard McKeon in his *Selections from Medieval Philosophers*, I (New York, 1929), 58–61.

Thus reason has perceived that numbers govern and make perfect all that is in rhythms (called "numbers" in Latin) and in song itself, has examined them diligently; and has found them to be eternal and divine. Next surveying heaven and earth, reason has perceived that in them only beauty pleases it, in beauty only figures, in figures dimensions, and in dimensions numbers. These things, separated and ordered, reason has brought together in a discipline which it calls Geometry. Profoundly impressed by the movement of the heavens, reason has been further prompted to inquire diligently into this. Through the endless succession of the seasons, through the harmonious and regular courses of the stars, through the orderly extent of the intervening distances, reason has perceived that, here too, only dimension and numbers hold sway. Similarly putting these things in order by defining and dividing, reason brought forth Astronomy. In this way, then, all things present themselves in the mathematical disciplines as harmonious, as having to do with the immortal numbers which are apprehended by reflection and study, those which are perceived by the senses being mere shadows and images.

Who, therefore, would say that the theory of numbers was transient or that any art could exist without it?

(D) That not only Music but also the three other disciplines exist by the authority of numbers seems now sufficiently suggested. So I beg you to begin to treat the nature of numbers more fully, repeating the single points which have gone before, so that by way of numbers I may somehow arrive at a comprehension of the innermost secrets of musical theory.

18. Franco of Cologne

The biography of this central figure among the medieval theorists is virtually a complete blank. That he was a papal chaplain and a praeceptor of the Cologne Commandery of the Hospital of St. John of Jerusalem is set forth at the end of his treatise; the Anonymous of the British Museum (Coussemaker's Anonymous IV), writing in the last quarter of the thirteenth century, stresses the importance of Franco's contributions to the improvement and standardization of mensural writing; in the second quarter of the century that followed, the venerable Jacob of Liége recalls having heard a motet of Franco's sung in Paris.

Franco's one genuine writing, the *Ars cantus mensurabilis*, rests to a considerable extent upon the work of the theorists who immediately preceded him, and its teachings are in effect a compromise between an ideally logical system and the existing practice. For nearly a century its authority was enormous and unrivalled: there were several abridged versions; its text was made the subject of a number of commentaries, among them one by Simon Tunstede; Marchetto da Padua and Jean de Muris took Franco as their point of departure; and in the *Speculum* of Jacob of Liége the Franconian notation and the music for which it was devised found their last but most persuasive advocate.

Ars cantus mensurabilis [1]

[*ca. 1260*]

PROLOGUE

Now THAT philosophers have treated sufficiently of plainsong and have fully explained it to us both theoretically and practically (theoretically

1 Text: Coussemaker, *Scriptores*, I, 117–135. On the authorship see Besseler in *Archiv für Musikwissenschaft*, VIII (1926), 157–158; on the date and musical examples, Ludwig, *ibid.*, V (1923), 289–291. Wherever possible, Coussemaker's examples have been corrected to agree with the compositions from which they come. The text has been emended here and there with the help of Burney's quotations from the text of the MS. Oxford, Bodl. 842 (*A General History of Music*, II, 179–192).

above all Boethius, practically on the other hand Guido Monachus and, as to the ecclesiastical tropes, especially the blessed Gregory); supposing plainsong to have been most perfectly transmitted by the philosophers already mentioned, we propose—in accordance with the entreaties of certain influential persons and without losing sight of the natural order—to treat of mensurable music, which plainsong precedes as the principal the subaltern.

Let no one say that we began this work out of arrogance or merely for our own convenience; but rather out of evident necessity, for the ready apprehension of our auditors and the most perfect instruction of all writers of mensurable music. For when we see many, both moderns and ancients, saying good things about mensurable music in their "arts" and on the other hand deficient and in error in many respects, especially in the details of the science, we think their opinions are to be assisted, lest perchance as a result of their deficiency and error the science be exposed to harm.

We accordingly propose to expound mensurable music in a compendium, in which we shall not hesitate to introduce things well said by others or to disprove and avoid their errors and, if we have discovered some new thing, to uphold and prove it with good reasons.

I. OF THE DEFINITION OF MENSURABLE MUSIC AND ITS SPECIES

Mensurable music is melody measured by long and short time intervals. To understand this definition, let us consider what measure is and what time is. Measure is an attribute showing the length and brevity of any mensurable melody. I say "mensurable," because in plainsong this kind of measure is not present. Time is the measure of actual sound as well as of the opposite, its omission, commonly called rest. I say "rest is measured by time," because if this were not the case two different melodies—one with rests, the other without—could not be proportionately accommodated to one another.

Mensurable music is divided into wholly and partly mensurable. Music wholly mensurable is discant, because discant is measured by time in all its parts. Music partly mensurable is organum, because organum is not measured in all its parts. The word "organum," be it known, is used in two senses—in its proper sense and in the sense commonly accepted.[2] For organum in its proper sense is organum duplum, also called organum

---

2 Cf. John of Garland (CS, I, 114a): "The word 'organum' is variously used—in a general sense and in a specific one"; Anonymous 4 (CS, I, 354b): " 'Organum' is an ambiguous word."

Wooldridge (*The Oxford History of Music*, I [1st ed., 1901], 177, 338–339) takes *organum communiter sumptum* to be a specific form.

purum. But in the sense commonly accepted organum is any ecclesiastical chant measured by time.

Since the simple precedes the complex, let us speak first of discant.

2. OF THE DEFINITION AND DIVISION OF DISCANT

Discant is a consonant combination of different melodies proportionately accommodated to one another by long, short, or still shorter sounds and expressed in writing as mutually proportioned by suitable figures. Discant is divided in this way: one kind is sounded simply; another, called hocket, is disconnected; another, called copula, is connected. Of these let us speak in turn. But since every discant is governed by mode let us explain first about the modes and afterwards about their signs or figures.

3. OF THE MODES OF EVERY DISCANT

Mode is the knowledge of sound measured by long and short time intervals. Different authorities count the modes differently, some allowing six, others seven.[3] We, however, allow only five, since to these five all others may be reduced.

The first mode proceeds entirely by longs. With it we combine the one which proceeds by long and breve—for two reasons: first, because the same rests are common to both; second, to put a stop to the controversy between the ancients and some of the moderns.[4] The second mode proceeds by breve and long, the third by long and two breves, the fourth by two breves and long, the fifth entirely by breves and semibreves.

But since sounds are the cause and principle of the modes, and notes are the signs of these, it is obvious that we ought to explain about notes, or about figures, which are the same. And since discant itself is governed both by actual sound and by the opposite, that is, by its omission,[5] and these two things are different, their signs are also different. And since actual sound precedes its omission, just as "habit" precedes "privation," let us speak of figures, which represent actual sound, before speaking of rests, which represent its omission.

---

3 John of Garland, who in this agrees with the authors of the *Discantus positio vulgaris* and *De musica libellus*, counts six modes (CS, I, 175a), adding (Jerome's text, CS, I, 97b): "Some add other modes, for example two longs and breve, but we need not count these, for with our six we have enough."

4 Cf. John of Garland (Jerome's text, CS, I, 98a): "Some would have it that our fifth mode is the first of all, and with good reason, for this mode precedes all the others. But as regards knowing the 'tempora,' the *modus rectus* takes precedence over the *modus obliquus;* thus the saying that the fifth mode is first does not hold." Pseudo-Aristotle (CS, I, 279a–281a) teaches a system of nine modes, beginning with Garland's fifth.

5 For the terms *vox recta* and *vox amissa* (or *omissa*) see John of Garland (CS, I, 176a) and Pseudo-Aristotle (CS, I, 278a); for the philosophical terms "habit" and "privation" Richard McKeon, *Selections from Medieval Philosophers,* II (New York, 1930), Glossary.

4. OF THE FIGURES OR SIGNS OF MENSURABLE MUSIC

A figure is a representation of a sound arranged in some mode. From this it follows that the figures ought to indicate the modes and not, as some have maintained, the contrary.[6] Figures are either simple or composite. The composite figures are the ligatures. Of simple figures there are three species—long, breve, and semibreve, the first of which has three varieties—perfect, imperfect, and duplex.

The perfect long is called first and principal, for in it all the others are included, to it also all the others are reducible. It is called perfect because it is measured by three "tempora," the ternary number being the most perfect number because it takes its name from the Holy Trinity, which is true and pure perfection. Its figure is quadrangular, with a descending tail on the right, representing length. ◥

The imperfect long has the same figure as the perfect, but signifies only two "tempora." It is called imperfect because it is never found except in combination with a preceding or following breve. From this it follows that those who call it "proper"[7] are in error, for that which is "proper" can stand by itself.

The duplex long, formed in this way: ◥ signifies two longs, combined in one figure in order that the line of plainsong in the tenor need not be broken up.

The breve, although it has two varieties, proper and altered, represents both by a quadrangular figure, without a tail: ■

Of the semibreve one variety is major, the other minor, although both are represented by the same lozenge-shaped figure: ◆

5. OF THE MUTUAL ARRANGEMENT OF FIGURES

Now the valuation of simple figures is dependent on their arrangement with respect to one another. This arrangement is understood, moreover, in that after a long follows either a long or a breve. Here be it also observed that the same is true of the valuation of breves and semibreves.

If long follow long, then the first long, whether it be a figure or a rest, is measured under one accent by three "tempora" and called perfect long:

---

6 This is at least implied by the definition of John of Garland (CS, I, 177b): "A figure is a representation of a sound according to its mode"; see also Pseudo-Aristotle (CS, I, 269b).

7 Cf. John of Garland (CS, I, 176a), who in this agrees with the author of the *De musica libellus* (CS, I, 378a).

But if breve follow long, the case is manifold, for there will be either a single breve or several of them.

If a single breve, then the long is of two "tempora" and called imperfect:

except between the two, namely between the long and the breve, there be placed that little stroke by some called "sign of perfection," by others "division of the mode." In this case, the first long is perfect, and the breve makes the following long imperfect:

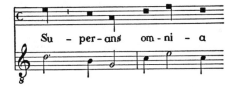

If several breves, the case is again manifold, for there will be two, three, four, five, or more than five.

If only two:

then the long is perfect, except a single breve precede it:

Of the two breves, the first, moreover, is called a breve próper, the second an altered breve. (A breve proper is one which contains one "tempus" only. An altered breve, while the same as the imperfect long in value, differs from it in form, for both, though differently figured, are measured by two "tempora." What we call a "tempus" is that which is a minimum in fullness of voice.) But if between the aforesaid two breves be placed the stroke called "division of the mode":

then the first long is imperfect and the second also, while the breves will both be proper. This, however, is most unusual.

If only three breves stand between the two longs:

the case is the same as before, except that the one which we called altered breve in the first instance is here divided into two breves proper. But if between the first breve and the two following ones there be placed a "division of the mode":

then the first long is made imperfect by the first breve, and of the two following breves the first becomes a breve proper while the last is altered. Observe also that three "tempora," whether under one accent or under several, constitute a perfection.

If more than three breves:

then the first long is always imperfect except the "sign of perfection" be
added to it:

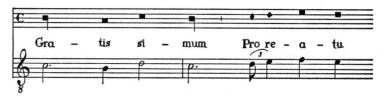

Of the following breves, all are proper that are found in counting by the
ternary number, which has been constituted perfection. But if at the end
only two remain, the second is an altered breve:

while if only one remains, it will be proper and will make the final long
imperfect:

Now the valuation of semibreves and breves is the same as in the rules
already given. But observe that there cannot stand for a breve proper
more than three semibreves (called minor semibreves, since they are the
smallest parts of the breve proper):

or less than two (of which the first is called a minor semibreve, the second
a major, since it includes in itself two minor ones):

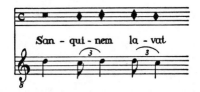

But if three semibreves follow immediately on two standing for a breve proper, or vice versa:

then let a "division of the mode" be placed between three and two, or vice versa, as shown in the preceding example. For an altered breve, moreover, there cannot stand less than four semibreves:

or more than six:

for the altered breve includes within itself two breves proper. From this appears the error of those who set for the altered breve at one time three semibreves and at other times two.

6. OF PLICAS IN SIMPLE FIGURES

Aside from these there are certain other simple figures, indicating the same things and called by the same names, but with the addition of what we call the plica.[8] Let us then consider what this is.

The plica is a note dividing the same sound into low and high. Plicas

---

[8] *Plica,* a fold, from *plicare,* to fold or double up.

are long, breve, and semibreve. But for the present we shall say nothing about the semibreve plica, for it cannot occur in simple figures, although, as will appear later on, it may be used in ligatures and groups of semibreves. Plicas, further, are either ascending or descending.

The long ascending plica is a quadrangular figure bearing on the right a single ascending stroke: ◢ or, more properly, bearing two strokes of which the right one is longer than the left: ⊔I say "more properly," for it is from these two strokes that the plica takes its name. The long descending plica likewise has two strokes, but descending ones, the right one longer than the left, as before: ⊓

The breve ascending plica is that which has two ascending strokes, the left one, however, longer than the right: ⊔ The descending breve plica has two descending strokes, the longer one on the left: ⊓

Observe also that these plicas have a force similar to that of the simple figures already mentioned and that they are similarly regulated as to value.

7. OF LIGATURES AND THEIR PROPERTIES

Simple figures having been discussed, let us speak about those that are composite or, what amounts to the same thing, bound together, those that are rightly called ligatures.

A ligature is a conjunction of simple figures duly ordered by strokes. Ligatures are either ascending or descending. In an ascending ligature the second note is higher than the first; in a descending ligature the first note is higher than the second. Ligatures, moreover, are said to be "with propriety," "without propriety," or "with opposite propriety." And this is with respect to the beginning of the ligature. With respect to the end, however, they are said to be either "with perfection" or "without perfection."

Observe also that these differences are essential and specific to the ligature themselves. Hence a ligature "with propriety" differs essentially from one that is "without," just as a rational being differs from an irrational one, and the same is true of the other differences we have mentioned. Species is subordinate to genus. Yet to the species themselves no name is given, but the differences we have mentioned and the genus to which they belong define them. This agrees with what occurs in other real genera: "animate body," for example, defines a certain species to which no name is given.

With respect to the middle notes of ligatures no essential difference is found, from which it follows that all middle notes in ligature agree in significance. Hence it appears that the position of those is false who hold that in the ternary ligature the middle note is a long,[9] although in all others it is a breve. Now let us consider what is meant by "with propriety," "without propriety," and "with opposite propriety," also by "with perfection" and "without perfection," and what the significance of all these things may be.

"Propriety" is the note at the beginning of a ligature of primary invention, borrowed from plainsong; "perfection" means the same thing, but with respect to the final note. Whence follow the rules of the differences we have mentioned.

Every descending ligature having a stroke descending from the left side of the first note is called "with propriety." being so figured in plainsong. If it lack the stroke it is "without propriety." Further, every ascending ligature is "with propriety" if it lack the stroke. If, however, it have a stroke descending from the left side of the first note, or from the right side, which is more proper, it is "without propriety."

Further, every ligature, whether ascending or descending, bearing a stroke ascending from the first note, is "with opposite propriety."

Now with respect to the final note of a ligature these rules are given. Every ligature bearing the final note immediately above the penultimate is "perfect." A ligature is made "imperfect" in two ways: first, if the final note be rectangular, without a plica, the head turned away from (instead of being above) the penultimate; second, if the last two notes be combined in one oblique form, ascending or descending. In ascent, however, this last "imperfection" is out of use, nor is it necessary except, as will appear later on,[10] when the final breve in an ascending ligature is to take a plica.

Aside from these things be it known that, just as by these differences one ligature differs from another in form, so also in value. Whence follow the rules of every ligature.

In every ligature "with propriety" the first note is a breve, in every one "without propriety," a long. In every ligature "with perfection" the final note is a long, in every one "without perfection," a breve. In every ligature "with opposite propriety" the first note is a semibreve, to which we add, "and the following one," not in itself, but in consequence, for no semibreve may occur alone. Further, every middle note is a breve, except, as already explained, it be made a semibreve by "opposite propriety." Be it also understood that in ligatures the longs are made perfect

9 Cf. John of Garland (CS, I, 179a–179b) on the expression of his second and fifth modes in ligature.

10 Page 149 below.

in the way that was explained under simple figures and that the breves in a similar way become proper or are altered.

8. OF PLICAS IN COMPOSITE FIGURES

Aside from this be it known that any ligature, whether perfect or imperfect, may take the plica, and this with respect to its end. (What a plica is, has already been explained under simple figures.) For perfect ligatures may take the plica in two ways, ascending or descending. Imperfect ligatures may also take the plica in two ways. And observe that imperfect ligatures always take the plica in oblique imperfection, ascending or descending. And in such a case, where an imperfect ligature is to take a plica, the oblique form must be used in ascending, because the final note is to be made a breve. For if the rectangular imperfection take the plica, the plica will make it perfect, since it shares the rule of perfection.[11] Without the plica, the oblique imperfection is not to be used, for the position of rectangular imperfection suffices wherever there is no plica and is more proper and more usual. With this the plicas of all ligatures are manifest.

There are also certain combinations of simple figures and ligatures which share the nature, in part of ligatures, in part of simple figures, and which cannot be called either the one or the other.[12] For the valuation of such combinations we can give no rules other than those already given for simple figures and ligatures. Besides, there are other arrangements of simple figures and ligatures, distinguished by the rules of simple figures alone, which supply the defect of the combinations not governed by rule.

9. OF RESTS AND OF HOW THROUGH THEIR AGENCY
THE MODES ARE CHANGED FROM ONE TO ANOTHER

The signs signifying actual sound having been discussed, let us consider the rests, which represent its omission. A rest is an omission of actual sound in the quantity proper to some mode. Of rests there are six species: perfect long, imperfect long (under which is included the altered breve, since they comprehend the same measure), breve proper, major semibreve, minor semibreve, and double bar (*finis punctorum*).

The rest of the perfect long is the omission of a perfect actual sound, comprehending in itself three "tempora." The rest of the imperfect long and altered breve is measured in a similar way by two "tempora" only.

---

11 That is, will give it the appearance of a long, being to the right, as in the long plica.

12 Franco refers here to the so-called *conjunctae,* conventional combinations derived from the *climacus* and other similar neumes, which appear to the theorists of the mensural notation to be made up of longs and semibreves, or of ligatures and semibreves.

The rest of the breve is the omission of a breve proper, including in itself a single "tempus." The major semibreve omits two parts of the breve proper, the minor a third part only. The double bar is called immensurable, for it occurs also in plainsong. This signifies simply that regardless of the mode the penultimate note is a long, even though it would be a breve if the mode were considered.

Aside from this, these six rests are subtly designated by six strokes, also called rests. Of these the first, called perfect, touching four lines, comprehends three spaces, since it is measured by three "tempora." For the same reason the imperfect rest, touching three lines, covers two spaces, the breve rest one space, the major semibreve rest two parts of one space, the minor semibreve rest one part only. The double bar, touching all lines, comprehends four spaces.

The formulae for all these are shown in the following example:

Observe also that rests have a marvelous power, for through their agency the modes are transformed from one to another. The proper rest of the first mode is the breve proper or perfect long; that of the second the imperfect long; those of the third and fourth properly perfect longs, though improperly breves proper or altered; the fifth ought properly to have the breve or semibreve. Now if the first mode, which proceeds by long, breve, and long, has after a breve an imperfect long rest:

it is changed to the second. If the second mode, after a long, takes a breve rest:

it is changed to the first.[13]

---

13 As Ludwig observes (*loc. cit.*, p. 290), these examples are poorly chosen: the mode does not change at all; it is simply that the form with up-beat is substituted for the form without. At the same time, the examples reveal the same confusion between quantity and accent that prompted the recognition of the fourth mode as a distinct variety of musical meter.

The fifth mode, when combined with the first in any discant, is governed by the rests of the first and takes a long note before a rest:

When combined with the second, it is governed by the rests of the second and takes a breve at the end before the rest:

When it is neither the one nor the other, it is governed by its own rests:

Observe also that all the modes may run together in a single discant, for through perfections all are reduced to one. Nor need one attempt to determine the mode to which such a discant belongs, although it may be said to belong to the one in which it chiefly or frequently remains.

Of rests and of the changing of the modes let these things suffice for the present.

10. HOW MANY FIGURES CAN BE BOUND AT ONE TIME?

Be it known that not to bind a figure that can be bound is a fault, but to bind a figure that cannot be bound a greater fault. Whence be it observed that longs cannot be bound together except in the binary ligature that is "without propriety" and "with perfection." Nor is it a fault if even in this situation they be unbound, for nowhere else are longs bound together. From this it follows that those who occasionally bind three longs together, as in tenors, err exceedingly, as do those who bind a long between two breves,[14] since, as we have seen, all middle notes become breves by rule.

14 Cf. p. 148 above and note 9.

Similarly, at one time more than two semibreves cannot be bound together, and then only at the beginning of the ligature, by which understand "of the ligature proper to semibreves."

Breves can be bound at the beginning, in the middle, and at the end.

From these things it is evident that, except the mode which proceeds
entirely by longs, any mode taken without words can be bound.

The first mode, which proceeds by long and breve, first binds three
"without propriety and with perfection," then two "with propriety and
perfection," and as many more twos as desired, so that it concludes with
two of this species, except the mode be changed.

Observe also that, as already explained under rests, the modes can be
changed in several ways.

The second mode takes a binary ligature "with propriety and perfection," then two, two, and so forth, of the same species, a single breve remaining, except the mode be changed.

The third mode takes a four-note ligature "without propriety and with
perfection," then three "with propriety and perfection," then three, three,
and so forth, except the mode be changed.

The fourth mode first binds three "with propriety and perfection," then
three, three, and so forth, of the same species, concluding with two "with
propriety and without perfection," except the mode be changed.

The fifth mode ought to be bound as far as possible, concluding with
breves or semibreves, except the mode be changed.

II. OF DISCANT AND ITS SPECIES

Figures and rests having been considered, let us speak of how discant
ought to be written and of its species. But since every discant is governed
by consonances, let us first consider the consonances and dissonances that
are sounded at the same time and in different voices.[15]

By concord we mean two or more sounds so sounded at one time that
the ear perceives them to agree with one another. By discord we mean the
opposite, namely, two sounds so combined that the ear perceives them to
be dissonant.

Of concords there are three species: perfect, imperfect, and intermediate.

---

15 Franco's treatment of concord and discord
is taken over, almost word for word, from John of
Garland (Jerome's text, CS, I, 104b–106a). But,
whereas Garland distinguishes three species of
discord: perfect, imperfect, and intermediate—
the intermediate discords ("which agree in part
with the perfect, in part with the imperfect")

being the tone and the diapente plus semitone—
Franco distinguishes only two, assigning the tone
to the imperfect species, the diapente plus semitone to the perfect. As to Garland's classification
of the concords, this goes back in turn to the *De
musica libellus* (CS, I, 382b).

Concords are perfect when two sounds are so combined that, because of the consonance, one is scarcely perceived to differ from the other. Of these there are two: unison and diapason.

Concords are imperfect when the ear perceives that two sounds differ considerably, yet are not discordant. Of these there are two: ditone and semiditone.

Concords are intermediate when two sounds are so combined that they produce a concord better than the imperfect, yet not better than the perfect. Of these there are two: diapente and diatessaron.

As to why one concord is more concordant than another, let this be left to plainsong.

Of discords there are two species: perfect and imperfect.

Discords are perfect when two sounds are so combined that the ear perceives them to disagree with one another. Of these there are four: semitone, tritone, ditone plus diapente, and semitone plus diapente.

Discords are imperfect when the ear perceives that two sounds agree with one another to a certain extent, yet are discordant. Of these there are three: tone, tone plus diapente, and semiditone plus diapente.

Observe also that both concords and discords can be endlessly extended, as in diapente plus diapason and diatessaron plus diapason, and similarly by adding the double and triple diapason, if it be possible for the voice.

Be it also known that immediately before a concord any imperfect discord concords well.

Discant is written either with words or with and without words. If with words, there are two possibilities—with a single text or with several texts. Discant is written with a single text in the cantilena, in the rondellus, and in any ecclesiastical chant. It is written with several texts in motets which have a triplum or a tenor, for the tenor is the equivalent of some text. It is written with and without words in the conduct and in the ecclesiastical discant improperly [16] called organum.

Observe also that except in conducts the procedure is the same in all these forms, for in all except the conduct there is first taken some cantus prius factus (called tenor, since it supports the discant and has its place from it). In the conduct, however, this is not the case, for cantus and discant are written by the same person. The word "discant," however, is used in two senses—first, as meaning something sung by several persons; second, as meaning something based on a cantus.

16 *Improprie,* Coussemaker's reading, is confirmed by Anonymous 1 (CS, I, 302b) and Jacob of Liége (CS, II, 395a), while Gerbert (GS, III, 12a) and Simon Tunstede (CS, IV, 294b and III, 361b) have *proprie.* If *improprie* is correct, the "ecclesiastical discant written with and without words" is organum "in the sense commonly accepted," not organum purum or duplum (cf. pp. 140–141 above).

In the former the procedure is as follows. The discant begins either in unison with the tenor:

or at the diapason:

or at the diapente:

or at the diatessaron:

or at the ditone:

or at the semiditone:

proceeding then by concords, sometimes introducing discords in suitable places, so that when the tenor ascends the discant descends, and vice versa. Be it also known that sometimes, to enhance the beauty of a composition, the tenor and discant ascend and descend together:

Be it also understood that in all the modes concords are always to be used at the beginning of a perfection, whether this beginning be a long, a breve, or a semibreve.

In conducts the procedure is different, for he who wishes to write a conduct ought first to invent as beautiful a melody as he can, then, as previously explained, using it as a tenor is used in writing discant.

He who shall wish to construct a triplum ought to have the tenor and discant in mind, so that if the triplum be discordant with the tenor, it will not be discordant with the discant, and vice versa. And let him proceed further by concords, ascending or descending now with the tenor, now with the discant, so that his triplum is not always with either one alone:

He who shall wish to construct a quadruplum or quintuplum ought to have in mind the melodies already written, so that if it be discordant with one, it will be in concord with the others. Nor ought it always to ascend or descend with any one of these, but now with the tenor, now with the discant, and so forth.

Be it observed also that in discant, as also in tripla and so forth, the equivalence in the perfections of longs, breves, and semibreves ought always to be borne in mind, so that there may be as many perfections in the discant, triplum, and so forth, as there are in the tenor, and vice versa, counting both actual sounds and their omissions as far as the penultimate, where such measure is not present, there being rather a point of organum here.

Of discant sounded simply let these things suffice for the present.

12. OF COPULA

A copula is a rapid, connected discant, either bound or unbound.

A bound copula is one which begins with a simple long and proceeds by binary ligatures "with propriety and perfection," as in the second mode, although it differs from the second mode in notation and in performance. It differs in notation, since the second mode does not begin with a simple long as the copula does:

If between the initial long and the following ligature be placed a division of the mode, it is no longer a copula, but is said to be in the second mode:

A –   men

In performance it differs also, since the second mode is performed with breve proper and imperfect long, while the copula is performed quickly to the end, as though with semibreve and breve.

An unbound copula is effected after the manner of the fifth mode, although it differs from the fifth mode in two respects—in notation and in performance. It differs in notation, since the fifth mode can be bound wherever there are no words, while the copula, although it is never used with words, is unbound:

A —   men

In performance it differs also, since the fifth mode is performed with breves proper, while the copula is more quickly connected in performance.

Of copula let these things suffice.

13. OF HOCKET

A truncation is a sort of music sounded in a broken way by actual sounds and their omissions. Be it also known that a truncation can be effected in as many ways as the long, breve, and semibreve can be divided.

The long is divisible in numerous ways. First, it can be divided into long and breve, or breve and long, and from this division a truncation or hocket (for this is the same thing) is so effected that in one voice a breve is omitted, in the other a long:

(In seculum)

Then it can also be divided into three breves, or two, and into several semibreves, and from all these divisions a truncation is so sung by actual sounds and their omissions that when one voice rests, the other does not, and vice versa.

The breve, on the other hand, can be divided into three semibreves or two, and from this division a hocket is sung by omitting a semibreve in one voice and performing one in the other:

Be it also observed that from these truncations, by the omission and sounding of longs and breves, are made the vernacular hockets. Be it also observed that in them all the equivalence of the "tempora" and the concord of the actual sounds ought to be borne in mind. Be it also known that every truncation ought to be based on a cantus prius factus, whether it be vernacular or Latin.

Of hocket let this suffice.

14. OF ORGANUM

Organum, in the proper sense of the word, is a sort of music not measured in all its parts. Be it known that there can be no organum purum unless the tenor sustain a single tone,[17] for when the tenor takes several tones in succession, discant begins at once:

[Constan - - tes e - sto - - te]

The longs and breves of organum are distinguished by three rules.[18] The first is: Whatever is written as a simple long note is long; as a breve, short; as a semibreve, still shorter. The second is: Whatever is long requires concord with respect to the tenor; if a long occur as a discord, let the tenor be silent or feign concord:[19]

[Ju - dea]

---

17 Literally, "Except over a tenor where a single note is in unison."
18 Cf. John of Garland (CS, I, 114b).
19 Cf. Garland's commentator, Anonymous 4

(CS, I, 362b): "Ii (the organum) be concordant, the tenor will sing out; if not, the tenor will be silent or quiescent."

The third is: Whatever occurs immediately before the rest which we call double bar is long, for every penultimate is long.

Be it also observed that in organum purum, whenever several similar figures occur in unison, only the first is to be sounded; let all the rest observe the florid style.[20]

Of discant and its species, of signs (that is, of figures and rests), and of organum let the things said here suffice.

Here ends the great "Art of music" of that reverend man, Dominus Franco, Papal Chaplain and Praeceptor of the Cologne Commandery of the Hospital of St. John of Jerusalem.

---

20 Cf. *ibid.*, (CS, I, 363a): "Two notes of the same pitch, whether concordant or not, represent the florid long."

19. Marchetto da Padua

An elder contemporary of Jacopo da Bologna and Giovanni da Cascia, a native of Padua and later a resident of Cesena in the Romagna, Marchetto is the principal spokesman for the musicians of the Italian Trecento. In his chief writings, the *Lucidarium* (on plainsong) and the *Pomerium* (on mensural music), written in 1318, we have a full account of the state of musical knowledge in Italy at the beginning of the fourteenth century, with useful observations on the current practice of Marchetto's fellow countrymen and on the contemporary French practice. The *Pomerium*, in particular, provides us with our earliest theoretical exposition of duple time as an equally privileged variety of musical measure; in addition, it shows us clearly that, however much the musicians of fourteenth-century Italy may have been dependent upon France, they were in no way dependent upon the theory of the French Ars Nova, as first formulated in 1319 by Jean de Muris.

From the Pomerium [1]

[1318]

Book II

OF IMPERFECT TIME

SEEING THAT musical discipline has to do with opposites, now that we have considered perfect time in mensurable music, let us also, in a similar way, consider imperfect time. And in considering it, let us proceed in this order. We shall treat: first, of imperfect time in itself and absolutely, in so far as the comprehension of its essence is concerned; second, of imperfect

1 Text: Gerbert, *Scriptores*, III, 170–178, the musical examples from Marchetto's *Brevis compilatio*, Coussemaker, *Scriptores*, III, 5–8. For the date see the present editor's "Intorno a Marchetto da Padua," in the *Rassegna musicale* for October 1950.

time in its application to notes according to its totality and multiplication; third, of imperfect time in its application to notes according to its partibility and division.

I. OF IMPERFECT TIME IN ITSELF AND ABSOLUTELY

1. What imperfect time is, speaking musically.

In the first place we say that imperfect musical mensurable time is that which is a minimum, not in fullness, but in semi-fullness of voice. This definition we demonstrate as follows. It is certain that just as the perfect is that which lacks nothing,[2] so the imperfect is that which lacks something. But it is also certain, by the definition of perfect time already demonstrated, that perfect time is that which is a minimum in entire fullness of voice, formed in the manner there expounded.[3] It follows, therefore, that imperfect time, since it falls short of perfect, is not formed in entire fullness of voice.

But someone may say: You ought to derive the deficiency of imperfect time with respect to perfect, not from fullness of voice, but from lessness of time. Whence you ought to say that both times, perfect as well as imperfect, are formed in fullness of voice, but that fullness of voice is formed in less time when it is formed in imperfect time than when it is formed in perfect. Whence (our opponents say) that minimum which is formed in fullness of voice is imperfect time, not perfect.

But to this we reply that to be in fullness of voice and to be a minimum is necessarily perfect time, for perfect musical time is the first measure of all, for which reason also the measure of imperfect time is derived from it by subtracting a part, as will presently be explained. Therefore, since the minimum in any genus is the measure of all other things in it, as previously observed,[4] we conclude that minimum time is always perfect of itself, provided it be formed in fullness of voice, for as soon as we subtract from the quantity of perfect time we constitute imperfect. And so it appears that to define time by fullness of voice is to define it by essential excess or deficiency. Therefore our definition stands, namely that imperfect time is that which is a minimum, not in fullness of voice, but in semi-fullness. This much in the first place.

2. How are perfect and imperfect time essentially opposed?

In themselves, absolutely, and without reference to any division or multiplication of either, perfect and imperfect time are essentially op-

---

2 Cf. Aristotle, *Metaphysics,* 1021B: "For each thing, and every substance, is perfect when, and only when, in respect of the form of its peculiar excellence, it lacks no particle of its natural magnitude." [Tredennick]

3 Cf. GS, III, 137b, where Marchetto names Franco as his authority for this definition.
4 Cf. GS, III, 137b, where Marchetto refers this statement to the authority of Aristotle.

posed, as is sufficiently clear from our definition. Nevertheless we also demonstrate this. It is certain that perfect and imperfect time are not wholly the same thing, for if they were, imperfect time could be called essentially perfect, and vice versa. Therefore they differ essentially. Now if two things differ essentially they differ actually, for the one is not the other. In this case they are opposed through "privation," for the one actually has something that the other has not. And from this it follows also that they are contradictory, for they can never both be true of the same thing at the same time. There can, then, be no time which could at once be essentially and actually perfect and imperfect.

And if someone say: Some time will be given which for various reasons will at once be perfect and imperfect; we reply that something or nothing will correspond to these reasons. If nothing corresponds, so much for the objection; if something, then one thing will at once be two things, which is impossible. It is therefore impossible for any musical time to be at once actually and essentially perfect and imperfect, as some pretend, for this implies a manifest contradiction, since it amounts to saying that someone is at once "man" and "not-man." And this much in the second place.

3. By how much does imperfect time fall short of perfect?

Imperfect time falls short of perfect by a third part, something we demonstrate as follows. It is certain that imperfect time is not as great in quantity as perfect, for if it were, it would not be imperfect. It is there-fore necessary that it fall short of it by some quantity. It can, moreover, not fall short by less than one part, for if you say "by half a part," that half a part will be one part, even though it would be half of the remainder. Therefore, since the primary and principal parts of perfect time are three, for it was divided above by ternary division to obtain what is primary and principal, if imperfect time fall short of perfect, it cannot do so by less than a third part. It follows, therefore, that imperfect time in itself and es-sentially comprehends only two parts of perfect time.

II. OF THE APPLICATION OF IMPERFECT TIME TO NOTES ACCORDING TO ITS TOTALITY AND MULTIPLICATION

In itself and according to its totality and multiplication, imperfect time is in its application to notes wholly similar in every respect to perfect. Notes of three "tempora," of two "tempora," and of one "tempus" occur in the same way in imperfect time as in perfect and are also similarly figured. All accidents of music in imperfect time, such as rests, tails, and dots, are situated just as in perfect.

The reason is this: Since there can never be a material science, nor yet a sensible knowledge, of imperfect things, except by comparison to perfect (for never, whether through the intellect or through the senses, can we know a thing to be imperfect except we also know what is needed to make it perfect); so science, as regards those things that are apprehended by the intellect or the senses, has always to do with the perfect. Music, therefore, both with regard to its notes and with regard to its accidents, has always to do primarily and principally with perfect time. But by a subtraction made by the intellect of a part, namely of perfect time, music becomes a science of imperfect time. For if imperfect time were to have its own notes and accidents, different from those of perfect time, it follows that there would be primarily and principally a science and a sensible knowledge of imperfect things, having no relation to the perfect, something which, as we have said, is impossible both according to the intellect and according to the senses.

And if someone says: Very well, I shall be guided by the perfect, namely by comparing to its notes and accidents those of imperfect time; we reply that this will be in vain, for by such a comparison he can satisfy only in the notes and accidents of perfect time, namely by subtracting fullness and in consequence quantity from them. Thus he would make notes and accidents of imperfect time in vain.

But he may ask: How am I to know when music is in perfect time and when in imperfect if, as you say, they are completely alike, both in their notes and in their accidents? We reply that this is to be left entirely to the judgment of the composer, who understands the science of music thoroughly. In order, however, that one may know what the wish of the composer is, when music is to be sung in perfect time and when in imperfect, we say that when they are combined some sign ought to be added at the beginning of the music so that by means of it the wish of the composer who has arranged this varied music may be known. For as concerns the figured music and the notes no natural difference can be discovered.

It is demonstrated that any written composition can be written either in perfect time or in imperfect, for this difference in the manner of singing it is provided by the composer, namely for the sake of the harmony, and is not derived from the nature of the music. For this reason a sign indicating the difference need be added only when the composer so wishes, nor can any valid reason be found why one sign is preferable to another. For some use I and II to indicate the perfect and imperfect; others 3 and 2 to indicate the ternary and binary divisions of the "tempus"; others use other signs according to their good pleasure.

But since every composition of itself and naturally observes perfect time more than imperfect (for this is the reason why one is called perfect, the other imperfect), music is by its nature inclined, not toward imperfect time, but toward perfect. It is because of the wish of the composer and for the sake of harmony that music observes imperfect time, abandoning perfect, and for this reason be it observed that it is the composer who adds the sign indicating that his intention in the music is imperfect time.

III. OF THE APPLICATION OF IMPERFECT TIME TO NOTES ACCORDING TO ITS PARTIBILITY AND DIVISION

1. Into how many principal parts is imperfect time divided?

According to its partibility and division, imperfect time is so applied to notes that by primary division it is divided into two parts. Nor can it be divided into more, something we demonstrate as follows. In our first book it was demonstrated that by primary division perfect time is divided into three parts, no more, no less; we say "by primary and perfect division" for reasons already adduced. At the beginning of this second book it was also shown that imperfect time falls short of perfect and, as was likewise shown there, that it cannot fall short by less than a third part. There remain, then, two parts of imperfect time. It is clear, therefore, that by primary division imperfect time can be divided only into two parts, for otherwise it would in no respect fall short of perfect. And this is logical and appropriate, for just as to perfect time corresponds the more perfect division, which is into three, no more, no less, and this division comprehends all others; so to imperfect time corresponds the imperfect division, which is into two. And just as imperfect division is a part constituted within the ternary, so imperfect time is a part constituted within perfect.

By the first division of imperfect time there are then constituted two semibreves and not more [the "divisio binaria"]. These are equal, namely in value, and they equal two of the three semibreves of the first division of perfect time [the "divisio ternaria"]. For this reason they ought to be similarly figured, for they are equal to one another in value and in nature.

2. Of the binary division of imperfect time, according to the first way of dividing it.

But if either of the two semibreves be given a descending tail ♩♩•♩♪ ♩♩•♪♩ we go on to the second division of imperfect time [the "divisio quaternaria"], which is the division of each of our two parts into two others and not into three. For we have already explained and shown that

imperfect time first observes imperfect division; if afterwards we were to
divide our primary parts into three, it would to this end be necessary to
repeat about threes. First let us say, then, that our parts of imperfect time
are first divided into two others, making four. These four are equal in
nature, and they equal eight parts of the twelve-part division of perfect
time [the "divisio duodenaria perfecta"] ♩♩♩♩ . ♫♫ . But if of these four
only three be given, the Italian practice is that the final one, being the end,
will equal the first two. But if either one of the others be given a tail, the
final one and the one without a tail will retain their natural value, the one
with a tail equaling the two others "by art" (*via artis*) ♩♩♩·♩ ♫ ♩♩♩·♪ ♪ .
With three notes, two cannot be given tails, for the second one with a
tail would be meaningless. And with four notes, if we remain in this
division, it is unnecessary to give tails to any; if it be done, the note
with a tail will belong either to the ternary division of the primary parts,
which is the division of each of two into three [the "divisio senaria
imperfecta"], or to the third division of imperfect time, which is the
division of each of four into two [the "divisio octonaria"]. In this case the
proportion between the notes with ascending and descending tails and
those without, and between the final notes and the preceding ones, both "by
art" and "by nature," is arrived at throughout as plainly demonstrated in
our chapter on the semibreves of perfect time, and they will also be given
the same names.

3. *On the secondary division of imperfect time.*

The principal parts of imperfect time, being two, can also be divided
each one into three, thus constituting six notes [the "divisio senaria imperfecta"], and these six can again be divided in twos, making twelve
[the "divisio duodenaria imperfecta"], or in threes, making eighteen [the
"divisio octodenaria imperfecta"]. In the manner in which they are
written and proportioned, in short, in all accidents and in their names,
these are similar to those of perfect time.

From what has just been said has arisen a not inconsiderable error in mensurable music. For some have said: You say that I can divide the two parts of
imperfect time in threes and thus have six. But these six have also been brought
about by dividing the three parts of perfect time in twos. Therefore (our critics
conclude) the "divisio senaria" is a mean between perfect and imperfect time.

We reply that, in dividing two things, a given number can always be found
in both, and yet no part of either can ever be a mean between the one thing and
the other; similarly, in dividing two lines by binary, ternary, and quaternary
division, a given division can always be found in both, and yet no part of either

can ever be a mean between the one line and the other. Thus, in dividing imperfect time into its parts, no matter how often you hit upon a number of parts which you arrived at in dividing perfect time into its parts, no part of imperfect time can ever be a mean between imperfect time and perfect, nor can all its parts together.[5]

And if someone says: You say that only the imperfect falls short of the perfect; we reply that this is true by the proportion of perfect time to imperfect, for in their essences the two times are distinct from one another, separate and opposite, as is clear from their opposed definitions, one being formed only in fullness of voice, the other in semi-fullness.

4. Of the disparity and difference between the French and the Italians when they sing in imperfect time, and of the question, which nation sings more rationally?

Be it known, moreover, that there is a great difference between the Italians and the French in the manner of proportioning notes in imperfect time, likewise in the manner of singing it. The Italians always attribute imperfection to the beginning, saying that the final note is more perfect, being the end. But the French say the opposite, namely that while this is true of perfect time; of imperfect time they say that the final note is always less perfect, being the end.

Which nation, then, sings more rationally? The French, we reply. The reason is that just as in anything perfect its last complement is said to be its perfection with respect to its end (for the perfect is that which lacks nothing, not only with respect to its beginning, but also with respect to its end), so in anything imperfect its imperfection and deficiency is understood with respect to its end (for a thing is called imperfect when it lacks something with respect to its end). If, therefore, we wish to sing or proportion sounds in the manner of singing in imperfect time, we ought rationally to attribute imperfection always to the final note, just as in the manner of singing in perfect time we attribute perfection to it. From this we conclude that in this manner of singing the French sing better and more reasonably than the Italians.

The manner of the Italians can, however, be sustained by saying that they imitate perfection in so far as they can (which is reasonable enough), namely by always reducing the imperfect to the perfect. Then, since the proportion of imperfect time is reduced to the perfection of perfect time (which amounts to reducing the imperfect to the perfect), the singing

---

[5] Cf. GS, III, 140b, where Marchetto resolves this confusion more simply: "Between contradictories there can never be a mean, according to the Philosopher; there can, then, never be a mean between perfect and imperfect time, speaking essentially, intrinsically, and *per se* of the nature of perfect and imperfect time." The reference is to Aristotle, *Metaphysics*, 1057A.

of the Italians in imperfect time can be sustained reasonably enough.

Be it said, however, that for the reason already given the French sing better and more properly.

5. Of the names and properties of the semibreves of imperfect time in the French and the Italian manner.[6]

If two semibreves be taken for the imperfect "tempus," in both the French and the Italian manner they are performed alike:

And since they are parts of the first division of imperfect time [the "divisio binaria"] they are called major semibreves "by nature," being comparable to two semibreves of the first division of perfect time [the "divisio ternaria"]. "By art," however, one of them can be given a tail; then in the Italian manner we go on to the second division of imperfect time [the "divisio quaternaria"], which is the division into four equal semibreves, and the semibreve with a tail, which is called major "by art," will contain three of four parts, the one without a tail retaining its natural value:

And since this second division of imperfect time is comparable in a partial way to the second division of perfect time [the "divisio senaria perfecta"], which is the division into six, its four equal semibreves are called minor semibreves "by nature."

But in the French manner, if one be given a tail, we go on at once to the ternary division of imperfect time [the "divisio senaria imperfecta"], which is

<hr />

6 Note that the French manner of dividing the imperfect "tempus," as described by Marchetto in this section, agrees throughout with that described by Philippe de Vitry in his *Ars nova* (CS, III, 18b–19a). But whereas de Vitry obtains his results "by art," Marchetto is chiefly concerned with a division "by nature"; his "French manner" corresponds roughly to that of the *Roman de Fauvel* (1314).

the division into six equal semibreves. These are called minims in the first degree, the semibreves having been divided beyond the division of minor semibreves. In this case the semibreve with a tail contains five of six parts "by art," the one without a tail retaining its natural value.

If three semibreves be taken for the imperfect "tempus," in the Italian manner the final one, being the end, will equal the two others in value:

But in the French manner, in order that the proportion and perfection of the whole measure may be preserved, the first note will contain three of six parts, the second two, and the third one, the notes being called major semibreve, minor semibreve, and minim.

When there are four semibreves, in the Italian manner they are performed alike:

But in the French manner (for in dividing imperfect time the French do not go beyond the "divisio senaria," even though they could) the first of these four contains two parts of six and the second one, the other two filling out the second half of the perfection in a similar way. This way of proportioning four notes among the six parts of the "tempus" was necessary in order that the French form might be generally observed. For, as will appear on reflection, in no other way can such a proportion or perfection be worked out without an excess or deficiency of perfection. For if each of the first two notes contain two of the "tempus," each of the remaining two containing only one, there will be no proportion between the parts, since in a division of this kind no mean proportion can ever rationally and naturally be found. This we call "by nature," for "by art" the same result can be obtained by adding the sign of art.

When there are five semibreves, in the Italian manner they belong to the third division of imperfect time [the "divisio octonaria"], which is the division into eight, comparable in a partial way to the division of per-

fect time into twelve [the "divisio duodenaria perfecta"], and the first
two will be called minims in the second degree, the others remaining in
the second division of imperfect time:

"By art," however, these minims can be placed otherwise among the five:

But in the French manner the first three are equal minims, the fourth containing two parts, the fifth one, for the French always place the more perfect
immediately before the less perfect, proportioning them one to the other. Thus
it ought always to be understood that the French attribute perfection to the
beginning.

When there are six semibreves, in the Italian manner the first four are
measured by four of eight parts of the "tempus," the last two remaining
in the second division:

"By art," namely by giving them ascending tails, the minims can be placed
otherwise:

But in the French manner all are equal and, as we have said before, they are called minims.

When there are seven semibreves, in the Italian manner the first six contain six parts of the "tempus," the last remaining in the second division:

except perchance it be artificially distinguished:

When there are eight semibreves, all are performed alike as minims:

But in the French manner, if one wished to take more than six semibreves for the imperfect "tempus," he would fall at once into its third division [the "divisio duodenaria imperfecta"], which is the division of six into twelve, and some of them would require ascending tails.

But he may ask: How can I know which of the semibreves with ascending tails belong to the third division, in twelve, and which to the second division, in six, when with six some are also given ascending tails in various ways? We reply that this depends on the number of notes being either less or greater than six.

And in order that it may be known which division of imperfect time we ought to follow in singing mensurable music, whether the French or the Italian, we say that at the beginning of any composition in the French

manner, above the sign of imperfect time which is placed there, there
should be placed a "G," denoting or indicating that the composition
should be performed in the French manner [7] (just as in plainsong the
founders of music placed a "Γ" at the beginning of the Guidonian hand to
show that we had music from the Greeks), for we had this division of the
imperfect "tempus" from the French. And if a single composition in imperfect time be proportioned according to the French and Italian manners
combined, we say that at the beginning of the part in the French manner
there should be placed a "G," but that in a similar way at the beginning
of the part in the Italian manner there should be placed a Greek "I"
["Y"], which is the initial of their name.

[7] For a clear example of Marchetto's "French manner," headed "s.g." (Senaria Gallica), see the caccia "Or quà conpagni" in W. T. Marrocco's *Fourteenth-Century Italian Cacce* (Cambridge, 1942), pp. 46–47 and plate IV.

20. Jean de Muris

A native of Normandy, Jean de Muris was born before 1300 and died about 1351. He is known to have taught at the Sorbonne in Paris. He was a man of great learning, a philosopher and mathematician whose interest in music was distinctly secondary. Jean de Muris was on friendly terms with Philippe de Vitry, whose *Ars nova* he energetically endorsed and defended in his writings. He is credited with the authorship of the important *Ars novae musicae* and with a few other writings. Ironically enough, the voluminous *Speculum musicae*, a violent attack on his teachings, passed until quite recently as one of his own writings.

From the Ars novae musicae [1]

[*1319*]

II. MUSICA PRACTICA

SEEING THAT in the preceding discourse [2] we have touched lightly and in brief on the theory of music, it now remains to inquire at greater length into its practice, that part which is mensurable, since different practitioners think differently about this. As was shown in Book I, sound is generated by motion, since it belongs to the class of successive things.[3] For this reason, while it exists when it is made, it no longer exists once it has been made. Succession does not exist without motion. Time inseparably unites motion. Therefore it follows necessarily that time is the measure of sound. Time is also the measure of motion. But for us time is the measure of sound prolonged in one continuous motion, and this same definition of time we give also to the single time interval.

---

1 Text: Gerbert, *Scriptores*, III, 292–297, 300–301. Some emendations have been obtained by collating Gerbert's text with Coussemaker's Anonymous VI (CS, III, 398–401) and with his text of the *Conclusiones* (*ibid.*, 109–113). On the

De Muris texts in general see Besseler in *Archiv für Musikwissenschaft*, VIII (1926), 207–209.
2 Gerbert, *Scriptores*, III, 312, 256–258, 313-315.
3 *Ibid.*, p. 256.

According to one account, there are two sorts of time—greater and lesser,[4] greater time having longer motion, lesser time shorter. These do not differ in species, other things remaining the same, for greatness and lessness do not alter species. But to every time interval of measured sound our predecessors reasonably attributed a certain mode of perfection, prescribing this sort of time interval in order that it might support a ternary division, for they believed all perfection to be in the ternary number. For this reason they prescribed perfect time as the measure of all music, knowing that it is unsuitable for the imperfect to be found in art. Yet certain moderns believe themselves to have discovered the opposite of this, which is not consistent. Their meaning will be more clearly set forth in what follows.

That all perfection is implicit in the ternary number follows from many likely conjectures. For in God, who is most perfect, there is one substance, yet three persons; He is threefold, yet one, and one, yet threefold; very great, therefore, is the correspondence of unity to trinity. At first, in knowledge, are the separate and the concrete; from these, under the ternary number, the composite is derived. At first, in celestial bodies, are the thing moving, the thing moved, and time. Three attributes in stars and sun—heat, light, splendor; in elements—action, passion, matter; in individuals—generation, corruption, dissolution; in all finite time—beginning, middle, end; in all curable disease—rise, climax, decline. Three intellectual operations; three terms in the syllogism; three figures in argument; three intrinsic principles of natural things; three potentialities of the being that has not suffered privation; three loci of correlative distance; three lines in the whole universe. After one the ternary number is the first that is odd; by multiplying it by itself three times is generated also the first incomposite cubic number. Not two lines, but three, enclose a surface; the source of all polygonic figures is the triangle; first of all rectilinears is the triangular. Every object, if it is ever to stand, has three dimensions.[5]

Now, since the ternary number is everywhere present in some form or other, it may no longer be doubted that it is perfect. And, by the contrary of this proposition, the binary number, since it falls short of the ternary, also since it is thus of lower rank, is left imperfect. But any composite number formed from these may properly be considered perfect because of its similarity and correspondence to the ternary. For time, since

---

4 Compare Philippe de Vitry (CS, III, 21b–22b), who enumerates three varieties of perfect time—least, medium, and greater—and two of imperfect—least and greater.

5 For the role of the number three in the musical theory of the Middle Ages see Hermann Abert, *Die Musikanschauung des Mittelalters* (Halle, 1905), pp. 179–181.

it belongs to the class of continuous things, is not only again divisible by ternary numbers, but is also endlessly divisible to infinity.

Seeing, on the other hand, that sound measured by time consists in the union of two forms, namely the natural and the mathematical, it follows that because of the one its division never ceases while because of the other its division must necessarily stop somewhere; for just as nature limits the magnitude and increase of all material things, so it also limits their minuteness and decrease. For it is demonstrated naturally that nature is limited by a maximum and a minimum; sound, moreover, is in itself a natural form to which quantity is artificially attributed; it is necessary, therefore, for there to be limits of division beyond which no sound however fleeting may go. These limits we wish to apprehend by reason.

Prolonged sound measured by definite time is formed in the air not so much in the likeness of a point, line, or surface, as rather conically and spherically (in the likeness of a sphere, as light is formed in free space), something which may be tested by six listeners placed according to the six differences of proportion. And since such a sound is set in motion by the effort of the person striking, which is finite, for it proceeds from a finite being, its duration and continuation are necessarily limited, for sound cannot be generated in infinity or in an instant. Its limits are disposed in this way.

All music, especially mensurable music, is founded in perfection, combining in itself number and sound. The number, moreover, which musicians consider perfect in music is, as follows from what has been said, the ternary number. Music, then, takes its origin from the ternary number. The ternary number multiplied by itself produces nine; in a certain sense this ninefold number contains every other, for beyond nine there is always a return to the unit. Music, then, does not go beyond the nine-part number. Now the nine-part number again multiplied by itself produces 81, a product which is measured by the ternary number in three dimensions, just as sound is. For if we take three threes, two threes, and one three nine times, always multiplying the products again by three; then, as 3 times 3 produces 9, and 3 times 9 27, so 3 times 27 produces 81. From the unit, then, the third part of the ternary number, which is perfect, to 81, which is likewise perfect, these are, we say, the maximum and minimum limits of any whole sound, for the length of such a sound is included between these extremes. Within them, four distinct degrees of perfection may rationally be apportioned. This is done as follows.

No musical perfection exceeds the ternary number; it comprises and forms it. A perfection is that according to which something is called perfect. Perfect is that which is divisible into three equal parts, or into two unequal ones, of which the larger is twice the smaller. Unity, moreover, is indivisible and may be called neutral. In these, then, is comprehended the genus of divisibility, likewise of indivisibility. Now 81 is ternary and in this respect perfect; 54 is the corresponding binary number and in this respect imperfect; the corresponding unit is 27, making the perfect imperfect and the imperfect perfect. In these three numbers we distinguish the first degree; from 27 to 9 is the second; from 9 to 3 is the third; from 3 to 1 is the fourth; in any one of these we find again the perfect, imperfect, and neutral in the numbers 3, 2, and 1. There are then four degrees, no more, no less.

We have still to show by what figures, signs, or notes the things which we have said may be appropriately indicated or represented and by what words or names these may be called, for at this very time our doctors of music dispute daily with one another about this. And although signs are arbitrary, yet, since they should all be to a certain extent in mutual agreement, musicians ought to devise signs more appropriate to the sounds signified. In devising these, the wiser ancients long ago agreed and conceded that geometrical figures should be the signs of musical sounds.[6] Now the figure most suitable for writing music is the quadrilateral, for it arises from a single stroke of the pen, and in such a quadrilateral, as in a genus, all musical notes have their origin.[7] For the musical note is a quadrilateral figure arbitrarily representative of numbered sound measured by time. Moreover, the distinctions of this form are nine: rectangularity, equilaterality, the tail, the dot, the position, the right side, the left side, the upward direction, and the downward direction, as will be seen in the diagram to follow.

Now the ancients, while they wrote reasonably about the figures of the second and third degrees, had little to say about the first and fourth, although they made use of these remote degrees in their singing. For reasons which we shall pass over, their figures did not adequately represent what they sang. Nevertheless they gave us the means of accomplishing completely what they had incompletely accomplished. For they assumed the ternary and binary designated by a similar figure, the unit by a dissimilar one, inasmuch as the binary is closer to the ternary than the unit is.[8] Among things having a common symbol one passes more readily from one to another. And conversely.[9] From the ternary to the binary, that

---

6 Omitting *quos puncta . . . voluerunt appellare* with CS, III, 399b.

7 Omitting *per causam . . . explicatur* with CS, III, 399b.

8 Omitting *Quae autem . . . ut eadem* with CS, III, 399b.

9 Evidently a familiar axiom; in a different connection it is cited also by Jacob of Liége (CS, II, 420a).

is, from perfect to imperfect, and vice versa, one passes more readily than from the ternary to the unit; whatever the degree, therefore, the more similar figure ought to be common to those things the distinction between which is not perceived in themselves but is manifest rather in their relation to another thing. In the second degree, according to our predecessors, the quadrilateral, equilateral, rectangular figure with a tail to the right, ascending or descending, represents perfect and imperfect alike, that is, the ternary and binary. The same figure without a tail represents the unit in the second degree, the ternary and binary in the third. In this degree, on the other hand, the quadrilateral, equilateral, obtuse-angular figure represents the unit.

As to the first degree, the earlier authorities spoke about the binary and the unit, omitting the ternary or representing it by a figure similar to the one denoting the binary. In the fourth they abandoned the unit entirely or figured it implicitly in the ligatures. This is the last figure in the fourth degree, namely a quadrilateral, equilateral, obtuse-angular figure with a tail ascending. But in the first degree the first figure is similar to the second, namely a quadrilateral, non-equilateral, rectangular figure with a tail to the right, ascending or descending.

The differences of the first degree are between the non-equilateral figure and the equilateral; those of the second degree between the figure with a tail and the one without; those of the third between the rectangular figure and the obtuse-angular; those of the fourth between the obtuse-angular figure with a tail and the one without.

We have still to speak about the names of the figures which are called notes. In the first degree we may name them triplex long, duplex long, simplex long. In the second, following the terminology of the ancients, perfect long, imperfect long, breve. In the third, after the fashion of the preceding degree, perfect breve, imperfect breve, semibreve (so named not from equal division, but from being greater or lesser, so that the binary is called the greater part of three, the unit the lesser part, the lesser semibreve having been so called by the ancients also). In the fourth degree, following the terminology of the preceding ones, perfect semibreve, imperfect semibreve, least semibreve.

By others the notes are named otherwise, the same sense remaining. Omitting those of the first degree, which are named appropriately enough, we have long, semilong, breve, semibreve, minor, semiminor, minim. Or as follows, and more appropriately: longa, longior, longissima (that is, magna, major, maxima, beginning the comparison with the unit of the first degree); then, in the second, perfecta, imperfecta, brevis, brevior, brevissima (or parva), minor, minima.

First degree	◥ 81	◥ 54	◥ 27
(Major mode)	Triplex long	Duplex long	Simplex long
	Longissima	Longior	Longa
	Maxima	Major	Magna
Second degree	◥ 27	◥ 18	■ 9
(Mode)	Perfect long	Imperfect long	Breve
	Long	Semilong	Breve
	Perfecta	Imperfecta	Brevis
Third degree	■ 9	■ 6	◆ 3
(Time)	Perfect breve	Imperfect breve	Minor semi-breve
	Breve	Semibreve	Minor
	Brevis	Brevior	Brevissima
Fourth degree	◆ 3	◆ 2	◆ 1
(Prolation)	Perfect semi-breve	Imperfect semi-breve	Minim
	Minor	Semiminor	Minim
	Parva	Minor	Minima

Perfection and imperfection are represented, as we have said, by the same figure, just as there may be in several forms the same general material; the distinction between them the authorities attribute to five modes (*modi*), as is evident in the second degree, the one about which they had most to say. Just as long before long is perfect, so also before two breves, before three breves, before a dot, before a long rest, long is always valued as three "tempora." And this distinction is called "from place or position." Imperfection is recognized in two modes—by the preceding unit or by the following unit. What has been said of the second degree is to be understood of the other degrees in their own way.

In any one of these degrees there may be distinguished the following species (*species*) of melody: one entirely in perfect notes or with the binary preceding and the unit following—as though one mode, these are identical in their rests; a second with the unit preceding and the binary following; a third combining the first and second, namely with the perfect note preceding and two units following; a fourth made in the opposite way; a fifth composed entirely of units and their divisions.

Of rests and ligatures new things might be said, but as to them let what is found in the canons of the ancients be sufficient, except that rests may now be arranged in the four degrees.

At the end of this little work be it observed that music may combine perfect notes in imperfect time (for example, notes equal in value to three breviores) with imperfect notes in perfect time (for example, notes equal in value to two breves), for three binary values and two ternary ones are made equal in multiples of six. Thus three perfect binary values in imperfect time are as two imperfect ternary ones in perfect, and alternating one with another they are finally made equal by equal proportion.[10] And music is sung with perfect notes in perfect time, or with imperfect ones in imperfect, whichever is fitting.

Again, it is possible to separate and disjoin perfections, not continuing them, as when a single breve occurs between two perfect notes, yet, the breves having been gathered together, the whole is reduced to perfection.[11] For what can be sung can also be written down.

Moreover, there are many other new things latent in music which will appear altogether plausible to posterity.

In this "Ars musicae" are included some things as it were obscured by being left implicit which, were they made explicit, would stop ever so many now disputing together about certain conclusions. It will be useful, then, if we, more from love of the disputants than for novelty's sake, were to demonstrate in an elegant way the truth of some conclusions regarding which there is among the masters growing doubt. And let no invidious critic rise up against us if, preserving the modes and other things which will be apparent, and observing always the bounds set by the ancients, we are obliged to lay down rules.

These are the conclusions.

1. That the long may be made imperfect by the breve.
2. That the breve may be made imperfect by the semibreve.
3. That the semibreve may be made imperfect by the minim.
4. That the long may be made imperfect by the semibreve.

10 Probably the first theoretical mention of the so-called *aequipollentiae*, in representing which the practical music of the fourteenth century makes use of the red (or colored) note. A specific example of the combination here described is the motet "Thoma tibi obsequia," cited by De Muris himself at the end of the *Quaestiones* (GS, III, 306a, and CS, III, 106a) and by Philippe de Vitry in his *Ars nova* (CS, III, 21a). On this example see Johannes Wolf, *Geschichte der Mensural-Notation* (Leipzig, 1904), I, 142; the motet itself was contained in a MS once the property of Philip the Good, discussed by Eugènie Droz and Geneviève Thibault in *Revue de musicologie*, X (1926), 1–8, and by Heinrich Besseler in *Archiv für Musikwissenschaft*, VIII (1926). 235–241.

11 Probably the first theoretical mention of syncopation.

5. That the breve may be made imperfect by the minim.
6. That the minim may not be made imperfect.
7. That the altered breve may be made imperfect by the semibreve.
8. That the altered semibreve may be made imperfect by the minim.
9. That the "tempus" may be divided into any number of equal parts.

. . . . .

In these nine stated conclusions there are implicit many other special ones which application will make clear to the student.

Now, if these few things which we have said include anything which is seen to be inconsistent with truth, we ask you, venerable musicians (you in whom we have delighted because of music from earliest youth, for no science is hidden from him who knows music well), how far, from love of this work, you will correct and charitably tolerate our defects. For it is not possible for the mind of one man, unless he have an angelic intellect, to comprehend the whole truth of any science. Perhaps in the course of time there will happen to us what is now happening to the ancients, who believed that they held the end of music. Let no one say that we have concealed the state of music or its immutable end. For knowledge and opinion move in cycles, turning back on themselves in circles, as long as it pleases the supreme will of Him who has freely created and voluntarily segregated everything in this world.

21. Jacob of Liége

Since the publication in 1924 of Walter Grossmann's study of the introductory chapters of the treatise that follows, it has been generally recognized that the *Speculum musicae,* once supposed to be the work of Jean de Muris, is actually a violent attack on him, written sometime during the second quarter of the fourteenth century by a certain Jacob of Liége, about whom virtually nothing is known. Perhaps the most encyclopaedic of all medieval writings on music, the *Speculum* covers the entire range of the musical knowledge of its time; its last book, from which certain chapters are translated below, is at once an eloquent defence of the music of the Ars Antiqua and an impassioned tirade against the Ars Nova and all its works. As such, Jacob's *Speculum* becomes the prototype of Artusi's notorious attack on Monteverdi at the beginning of the seventeenth century.

From the Speculum musicae [1]

Prohemium to the Seventh Book

IN HIS commentary on the *Categories* of Aristotle, Simplicius says, commending the ancients: "We are not everywhere equal to discerning between true and false, yet in this we delight in attacking our betters." [2]

In this matter, just as it is profitable and praiseworthy to imitate things well done by the ancients, so it is pleasant and commendable to approve things well said by them, not to attack them, which last seems more the part of youths, for though youths are more inventive, old men are conceded more judicious. On this account, as the Master says in his *Histories,* youths and inexperienced persons, pleased by new things (for novelty is

---

1 Text: Coussemaker, *Scriptores,* II, 384–385, 427–432. On the authorship see Besseler in *Archiv für Musikwissenschaft,* VII (1925), 181.
2 *Commentaria in Aristotelem graeca,* VIII (Berlin, 1907), 8. I am indebted to my friend Dr. W. J. Wilson of the National Archives for the identification of this reference.

congenial and enchanting to the ear), ought not so to praise the new that the old is buried.[3] For as a rule new teachings, although on first acquaintance they glitter outwardly, are seen to lack solid foundations within when they are well examined, are rejected and do not last long. For the rest, if it be unprofitable to accomplish by many means what can conveniently be accomplished by few, what profit can there be in adding to a sound old doctrine a wanton and curious new one, repudiating the former?

For it is written: Thou shalt not remove thy neighbor's landmark, which they of old time have set.[4]

Long ago venerable men (among them Tubal Cain, before the flood) wrote reasonably on plainsong; since that time many more (of whom we have already made mention) have done the same while many others (among whom stands out Franco, the German [*Teutonicus*], and a certain author who goes by the name of Aristotle) [5] have written on mensurable music. Now in our day have come new and more recent authors, writing on mensurable music, little revering their ancestors, the ancient doctors; nay, rather changing their sound doctrine in many respects, corrupting, reproving, annulling it, they protest against it in word and deed when the civil and mannerly thing to do would be to imitate the ancients in what they said well and, in doubtful matters, to defend and expound them. Considering these things in the modern manner of singing and still more in the modern writings, I was grieved. Disposed, then, to write certain things about mensurable music with the defense of the ancients as my primary and principal purpose, I afterwards, as a secondary purpose and from necessity, turned to plainsong and to theoretical and practical music. Having with God's help completed what was incidental, let me now, if I can, carry out my original design.[6]

And at this point I ask the benevolent reader to spare me and beg him condescend to me, for to my regret I am alone, while those whom I attack in this last satiric and controversial work are many. Not that I doubt that the modern way of singing and what is written about it displease many worthy persons, but that I have not noticed that there is anything written against it. I still belong to the ancient company which some of the moderns call rude. I am old; they are young and vigorous. Those whom I defend are dead; those whom I attack still living. They

3 Possibly a reference to Aristotle, *Nicomachean Ethics*, I, iii, 5.

4 Deuteronomy 19:14.

5 Magister Lambert, whose *Tractatus de Musica* is published by Coussemaker as the "Quidam Aristoteles" (*Scriptores*, I, 251–281).

6 The first six books of the *Speculum*, here called "incidental," amount to 473 chapters alone; see the tables of contents in CS, II, xvii–xxii, 193–196.

rejoice in having found nine new conclusions about mensurable music; [7] in this I am content to defend the ancient ones, which I deem reasonable.

"For knowledge and opinion move in cycles," they say, borrowing from Aristotle's *Meteorology.* For now it is earth where before it was water. And we are not to ascribe the modern attack on the ancients to presumption, for it is made from love of truth and of piety besides, for the moderns say also that they write from love of truth.

Where there are two friends it is most sacred to honor truth. "Socrates is my friend, but truth is still more my friend." [8] Whence St. Jerome, in his epistle against Rufinus, says on the authority of Pythagoras, who in this was repeating a divine teaching: "Let us cultivate truth, which alone brings men close to God." [9] For he who deserts truth deserts God, since God is truth.

It still seems pious to honor the ancients, who have given us a foundation in mensurable music; pious to defend them in what they said well and, in doubtful matters, to expound them, not to attack them; uncivil and reprehensible to attack good men after they are dead and unable to defend themselves. Let what I have said be my apology. For though in this work I am about to speak against the teachings of the moderns (in so far as they oppose the teachings of the ancients), I delight in their persons and from my youth have delighted in song, singers, music, and musicians.

·   ·   ·   ·   ·

43. A COMPARISON OF THE OLD ART OF MEASURED MUSIC WITH THE NEW, AS REGARDS PERFECTION AND IMPERFECTION

At this point, as I near the end of this work, let me draw certain comparisons, not lacking weight, from what has been already said. May what I have said and shall further say be as it appears to me, without prejudice of any kind. The facts are in no way altered by any assertion or denial of mine. May what is reasonable or more reasonable and what accords more fully with this art be retained, and what is less reasonable be rejected. There must be place for what accords with reason and with art, since this lives by art and reason in every man. Reason follows the law of nature which God has implanted in rational creatures. But since imperfections have at last come to be discussed, let us compare the ancient art of measured music with the modern, in order to continue with our subject.

---

7 For this and the following references to the "moderns," cf. Jean de Muris, *Ars novae musicae* (pp. 178–179 above). The reference to Aristotle's *Meteorology* is to 339B.

8 Proverbial, but ultimately derived from Aristotle, *Nicomachean Ethics,* I, vi, 1.

9 Migne, *Patrologia latina,* XXIII, 507.

To some, perhaps, the modern art will seem more perfect than the ancient, because it seems subtler and more difficult: subtler, because it reaches out further and makes many additions to the old art, as appears in the notes and measures and modes; for the word "subtle" is used of that which is more penetrating, reaching out further. That it is more difficult may be seen in the manner of singing and of dividing the measure in the works of the moderns.

To others, however, the opposite seems true, for that art appears to be more perfect which follows its basic principle more closely and goes against it less. Now the art of measured music is based on perfection, as not only the ancients but the moderns [10] declare. Therefore whichever makes the greater use of perfection appears to be the more perfect; but this is true of the ancient art, the art of Master Franco.

For the new art, as we have seen, uses manifold and various imperfections in its notes, modes, and measures. Everywhere, as it were, imperfection enters into it: not content with this imperfection in notes, modes, and measures, it extends the imperfection to the time. For the new art has what it calls imperfect time, and has breves which it calls imperfect in regard to time, a thing unknown to the old art, and it applies an imperfection arising from time to the notes of the individual degrees.

Not content with simple, duplex, and triplex longs and with breves, and some not content even with semibreves, the practitioners of this art are still inventing new ways of corrupting what is perfect with many imperfections: proximate or direct, as when the perfect simple long is made imperfect by the breve; remote, when the same note is made imperfect by the semibreve because it is the third part of a breve recta; more remote, when the same long is made imperfect by the minim. Nor are the moderns satisfied with making perfect notes imperfect and dragging them to imperfection; they must do this also with the imperfect notes, since a single imperfection does not suffice them, but only many.[11]

If the new art spoke of the said imperfections only in a speculative way, it would be more tolerable; but not so, for they put imperfection too much into practice. They use more imperfect notes than perfect; more imperfect modes than perfect; and consequently more imperfect measures. So that when the new art is said to be subtler than the ancient, it must be said also that, granting this, it is not therefore more perfect.

For not all subtlety is proof of perfection, nor is greater subtlety proof of greater perfection. Subtlety has no place among the degrees or orders

---

10 Cf. Jean de Muris, *op. cit.* (p. 173 above). the conclusions of his *Ars novae musicae* (pp.
11 Cf. the terminology of Jean de Muris and 178–179 above).

or species of perfection, as is made clear in the fifth book of the *Metaphysics*,[12] nor is it sufficiently proved that the new art is subtler than the old. Even if we grant that it includes some new devices to which the old does not extend, the inclusion of many imperfections unknown to the old art does not prove it more perfect, but merely raises the question which of the arts under discussion is the more perfect.

As to the further assertion that the modern art is more difficult than the ancient, this, it must be said, does not make it more perfect, for what is more difficult is not for that simple reason more perfect. For though art is said to be concerned with what is difficult, it is nevertheless concerned with what is good and useful, since it is a virtue perfecting the soul through the medium of the intellect; for which reason authority says that the teaching of the wise is easy. But this will be discussed later on.

44. A COMPARISON OF THE OLD ART OF MEASURED MUSIC WITH THE NEW AS REGARDS SUBTLETY AND RUDENESS

Some moderns regard those singers as rude, idiotic, undiscerning, foolish, and ignorant who do not know the new art or who follow the old art, not the new, in singing, and in consequence they regard the old art as rude and, as it were, irrational, the new as subtle and rational. It may be asked, what is the source of this subtlety in the moderns and this rudeness in the ancients? For if subtlety comes from a greater and more penetrating intellect, who are to be reputed the subtler: those who discovered the principles of this art and found out what things are contrary to them, but have scrupulously followed these principles, or those who protest their intention of following them but do not, and seem rather to combat them? Let the judicious observe which party is offering a true judgment of this matter, without predilection, and what is the value of subtlety, what the value of difficulty, without utility. What is the value of subtlety which is contrary to the principles of science? Are not the subtlety and difficulty involved in the many diverse imperfections in notes, times, modes, and measures which they have contrived, incompatible with a science which is based on perfection? Is it great subtlety to abound in imperfections and to dismiss perfections?

Should the ancients be called rude for using perfections, the moderns subtle for using imperfections? Should the moderns be called subtle for introducing triplex longs, for joining duplex longs in ligature, for using duplex longs profusely, for using semibreves singly, for providing them

---

12 Aristotle, *Metaphysics*, 1021 B.

with tails, for giving them the power of making longs and breves imperfect and at the same time another power which seems unnecessary to this art,[13] and for many other innovations which seem to contradict its basic principle? Should they further be called subtle for their new manner of singing, in which the words are lost, the effect of good concord is lessened, and the measure, as will be discussed later on, is confounded? And who are those who use many distinct sorts of music and manners of singing, who apply themselves to many distinct sorts of music and manners of singing? Do not the moderns use motets and chansons almost exclusively, except for introducing hockets in their motets? They have abandoned many other sorts of music, which they do not use in their proper form as the ancients did; for example, measured organa, organa not measured throughout, and the organum purum and duplum, of which few of the moderns know; likewise conducts, which are so beautiful and full of delight, and which are so artful and delightful when duplex, triplex, or quadruplex; likewise duplex, contraduplex, triplex, and quadruplex hockets. Among these sorts of music the old singers divided their time in rotation; these they made their foundation; in these they exercised themselves; in these they delighted, not in motets and chansons alone. Should the men who composed and used these sorts of music, or those who know and use them, be called rude, idiotic, and ignorant of the art of singing? For although they do not sing the modern sorts of music or in the modern manner, and do not use the new art of the moderns, they would know that art if they were willing to give their hearts to it and sing in the modern manner, but the manner does not please them, only the ancient manner, perhaps for the reasons previously discussed or others which can be discussed.

One modern doctor [14] says thus: "The duplex long in the perfect mode takes up six tempora. In this Franco and Petrus de Cruce and all the others are wrong: it should really take up nine." This doctor seems to be denouncing not merely the ancients, of whom he names two of great merit, but the moderns as well, since in that remark he says that not merely those two but all the others are wrong. He does not say, "the ancients," but says absolutely, "all the others," and in consequence says that he himself is wrong. For if all those men are rude so far as they are in error according to the statement to which I have replied above, and according to certain

---

13 Cf. Jean de Muris, *op. cit.*, Conclusion 7: "The altered breve may be made imperfect by the semibreve" (p. 179 above).

14 An otherwise unknown theorist whom Jacob

has previously quoted and criticized in Chapters 26 and 27 of the present book of the *Speculum* (CS, II, 410a–412a).

other statements of his previously discussed, he is still more in error; but I think that like all the other doctors, he believed himself to be speaking truth.

The old art, it is clear, must not be considered rude and irrational; first, because the arguments brought against it and some of the additions made to it by the moderns have been previously shown to be respectively contrary to reason or unnecessary to art; secondly, because even if the moderns have made good additions to the ancient art, it does not follow that the ancient art is in itself rude and irrational and its inventors and practitioners the same. Thus, granted that the doctors who have succeeded Boethius, as the monk Guido and the rest, have made many good additions to the art of tones or modes which he transmitted to us, the art of Boethius and Boethius himself should not on that account be reputed rude and irrational. For he laid the foundations of the art and furnished the principles from which others, following him, have drawn good and useful conclusions, consonant with the art and not contrary to or incompatible with those principles.

For if the moderns make many distinctions and use many designations with regard to semibreves, the ancients, as has been mentioned, seem to use more, so far as the facts go, however it may be with regard to the shapes. For when they used for the same equal tempus, that is, for the breve in its proper sense, now two unequal semibreves, now three, now four, five, six, seven, eight, or nine equal ones, these could be called semibreves secundae when they used two, because two such were the equivalent of the breve; semibreves tertiae when they used three, because three such equalled the breve in value; semibreves quartae when they used four, for a similar reason; semibreves quintae, when five; semibreves sextae, when six; semibreves septimae, when seven; semibreves octavae, when eight; semibreves nonae, when nine, for a similar reason, as stated above.[15] Though they made all these distinctions in semibreves, they never distinguished them in their shape and never gave them tails, but distinguished them sufficiently from each other by means of points.

45. A COMPARISON OF THE ANCIENT ART OF MEASURED MUSIC WITH THE NEW AS REGARDS LIBERTY AND SERVITUDE

The art of singing of the moderns seems to compare with the ancient art as a lady with a bondwoman or a housemaid, for now the new art seems to be mistress, the old art to serve; the new art reigns, the ancient is exiled.

---

15 Cf. VII, xvii (CS, II, 400b–402b), in which Jacob gives examples from Petrus de Cruce and an anonymous, illustrating the use of from four to nine semibreves for the perfect breve.

But it is contrary to reason that the art which uses perfections should be reduced to subjection and the art which uses imperfections should dominate, since the master should be more perfect than the slave.

Again, these arts seem to compare with one another as the old law with the new, except that in this comparison the art of the moderns seems to be in the position of the old law and the old music in that of the new law. For the new law is freer, plainer, more perfect, and easier to fulfill, for the new law contains fewer precepts and is less burdensome to observe. Wherefore our Lord saith in the Gospel: "My yoke is easy and my burden is light." [16] And St. James in his Epistle: "Whoso looketh into the perfect law of liberty." [17]

But the old law contained many and diverse moral, judicial, and ceremonial precepts which were difficult to fulfill. Whence St. Peter, in the Acts of the Apostles, speaking of the old law: "Why tempt ye God, to put a yoke upon the neck of the disciples which neither our fathers nor we were able to bear?" [18]

The teachings of the old law of measured music are few and clear as compared with those of the new. It would take long to recount how the moderns use rules for their various longs, breves, and semibreves, for their various measures and modes of singing; how they lay down various instructions for causing imperfections; how they use rules in distinguishing their sorts of music; nor are they wholly in agreement in their doctrines. For some of them indicate perfect time in their music with a round circle, because the round form is perfect, whereas others use three little strokes to denote this. These three strokes must touch one line and project a little on each side, to distinguish them from the strokes that denote rests.[19] And the prescriber of this rule upbraids those who ignore it, counting them as idiots and witless. For since here is obviously great learning, here is great wisdom, and let these things be positive. And perfect and imperfect time may be distinguished from each other in another way or other ways than these if combined with one another.[20] To denote the perfect mode they set down a quadrangle enclosing three little strokes; but to denote the imperfect mode, they set down a quadrangle enclosing two little strokes.[21] Others, to denote the imperfect, place a sign made up of two semicircles, and by such a sign they denote both the time and the mode. And as one of them says, they do not know how to denote the one without the other. Others presume to prefix M for the perfect mode and

16 Matthew 11:30.
17 James 1:25.
18 Acts 15:10.
19 Cf. Philippe de Vitry, *Ars nova* (CS, III, 19b).

20 That is, by means of the red (or colored) note; cf. Philippe de Vitry, *op. cit.* (CS, III, 21).
21 *Ibid.* (CS, III, 20b–21a).

N for the imperfect, saying that as *O* and *C* are used for variation of time, so *M* and *N* are used for recognition of the mode. Others, as if reversing matters, understand by *O* the perfect mode and perfect time, but by *C* the imperfect mode and imperfect time. Others say that a circle enclosing three little strokes may be used for the perfect mode and time, but to designate the imperfect mode and time they set down a semicircle enclosing two little strokes.[22]

These things and many others which the ancients never used the moderns use, and thus they drag this art to many burdens, and she who before was free from these burdens now seems a bondwoman as regards such matters, whereas, according to Seneca, liberty is one of the greatest goods, for which reason the poet says:

> Not for all the gold in the world were liberty well sold.[23]

And since the old art is free from such burdens, the moderns do not permit her to rule. But since that is no right rule in which the free man who should be master is subject to him who is not free, the philosopher,[24] in his *Politics*, greatly disapproves of such government or rule.

46. A COMPARISON OF THE OLD ART OF MEASURED MUSIC WITH THE MODERN AS REGARDS STABILITY, AND OF THE OLD MODE OF SINGING WITH THE NEW

One important difference, among others, between perfect and imperfect work is that the perfect work is more stable than the imperfect; for the perfect work has no need of another; its existence does not depend on its being ordered with respect to something else; it has a firm foundation. That art, then, which is the more perfect of the two measured arts, the old and the modern, must be the one which is the more stable. Likewise, as has been mentioned above, we sometimes find certain new doctrines unstable, for though at first they are gladly and freely accepted because of their novelty, they displease and are rejected when well examined, lacking solid foundations, and there is a return to the more ancient teachers. Would it were thus with the modern measured art with respect to the old art!

For since the modern teachers are not fully in agreement with respect to the said art in their treatises, this is a sign of the instability of their art. For it is written that every kingdom divided against itself is brought to desolation,[25] for if one man oppose the other, how will their kingdom

---

22 *Ibid.* (CS, III, 21a).
23 Proverbial.
24 Aristotle.
25 Luke 11:17.

stand? Indeed if division spells evil and instability, then, according to the words of the prophet Hosea, their heart is divided; now shall they perish.[26]

Moreover, measured music seeks concord and shuns discord. It does not seek discordant teachers to attain these ends; indeed, all good things accord together. Would that it pleased the modern singers that the ancient music and the ancient manner of singing were again brought into use! For, if I may say so, the old art seems more perfect, more rational, more seemly, freer, simpler, and plainer. Music was originally discreet, seemly, simple, masculine, and of good morals; have not the moderns rendered it lascivious beyond measure? For this reason they have offended and are offending many judicious persons skilled also in music as Thales the Milesian offended the Spartans and Laconians,[27] a matter mentioned in our first book. Let the judicious take heed and decide what is true. For what purpose have the old music and method of singing and the practice of the old art been banished in favor of the moderns and the modern method of singing? What penalties had they incurred? Were they banished because of their goodness? But they do not please the satraps. As King Achish said to David: "Thou art upright and good, but thou dost not please the satraps." [28]

It is illegal that anyone should be an exile from his country save for sure and just cause, and that he should be cut off from the fellowship of the faithful, as if excommunicated, save by his own fault. I do not deny that the moderns have composed much good and beautiful music, but this is no reason why the ancients should be maligned and banished from the fellowship of singers. For one good thing does not oppose another, any more than one virtue opposes another.

In a certain company in which some able singers and judicious laymen were assembled, and where modern motets in the modern manner and some old ones were sung, I observed that even the laymen were better pleased with the ancient motets and the ancient manner than with the new. And even if the new manner pleased when it was a novelty, it does so no longer, but begins to displease many. So let the ancient music and the ancient manner of singing be brought back to their native land; let them come back into use; let the rational art once more flourish. It has been in exile, along with the corresponding method of singing, as if violently cast out from the fellowship of singers, but violence should not be perpetual. Wherein does this studied lasciviousness in singing so

---

26 Hosea 10:2.
27 Jacob seems to have confused Thales with Timotheus.
28 Cf. I Samuel 29:6.

greatly please, by which, as some think, the words are lost, the harmony of consonances is diminished, the value of the notes is changed, perfection is brought low, imperfection is exalted, and measure is confounded?

In a great company of judicious men, when motets in the modern manner were being sung, I observed that the question was asked, what language such singers were using, whether Hebrew, Greek, Latin, or some other, because it could not be made out what they were saying. Thus, although the moderns compose good and beautiful texts for their songs, they lose them by their manner of singing, since they are not understood.

This is what it has seemed needful to say in support of the old art of measured music and in defense of those who practice it. And since I have not found any previous teachers who have written of this matter, may I find successors and helpers who will write of it and will fortify with better arguments what I have touched upon.

Index